NAPOL
BOOK
FATE

The updated and revised version of
the Ancient Egyptian Oracle discovered
and used by Napoleon.

NAPOLEON'S BOOK OF FATE

Ancient Egyptian Fortune-Telling for Today

by
H. Kirchenhoffer
1822

Revised and edited by
Bonnie Parker

THE AQUARIAN PRESS
Wellingborough, Northamptonshire

This revised edition first published 1988

British Library Cataloguing in Publication Data

Napoleon's book of fate. — Rev. ed.
1. Astrology, Egyptian
I. Kirchenhoffer, H. II. Parker, Bonnie
III. Napoleon, *I, Emperor of the French*
133.5'0932 BF1714.E3/

ISBN 0-85030-684-1

The Aquarian Press is part of the Thorsons Publishing Group, Wellingborough, Northamptonshire, NN8 2RQ, England

Printed in Great Britain by Woolnough Bookbinding Limited, Irthlingborough, Northamptonshire

1 3 5 7 9 10 8 6 4 2

Contents

Acknowledgements

The author wishes to acknowledge the following: Carol Bellina and Monty Thrasher for the symbols used in the text; Wizards Bookshelf, Box 6600, San Diego, CA 92106 for extensive quotations from *The Divine Pymander of Hermes Mercurius Trismegistus*; and to the many others from whom I have used quotations.

To Mary Lee Caya

Introduction

> 'Each day's business is transacted according to the needs of the day. He claims to believe in Fate.' GENERAL JEAN BAPTISTE KLEBER

Two choices were open to the brilliant general, Napoleon Bonaparte, in the year 1798. He could have accepted command of a campaign against the English enemy on their own soil instead of the amazing expedition to Egypt. Had he not sailed to Egypt would his destiny — his *Fate* — marked him as brightly? Perhaps, perhaps not. Historians appear to agree that the English would have soundly defeated the French based on the strength of British manpower. Conjecture aside, Napoleon set sail from Toulon in May 1798 with over 400 ships. On board were a team of 175 astronomers, geometricians, mineralogists, chemists, antiquarians, bridge-builders, road engineers, orientalists, political economists, painters, poets and hundreds of boxes full of apparatus and books.

He was an avid student and reader. Alexander the Great was among his favourite historical personages. In Napoleon's notebook were frequent entries concerning Egypt and India. A penned quote from Raynal read, 'In view of the position of Egypt, lying betwixt two seas, and in fact betwixt the East and the West, Alexander the Great conceived the design of establishing the capital of his world-wide empire in that country, and of making Egypt the centre of world commerce'. (More current scientific calculations have proven the Great Pyramid to be located upon the exact centre of the land mass of earth.) Napoleon felt the English also believed in the wisdom of this statement and intended to damage their headway into commercial, political, and military control of the centre of the world. By July he defeated the Mamluks of Egypt in the Battle of the Pyramids near Cairo. He organized a modern government for Egypt, abolished feudalism, began irrigation projects, mapped out a Suez Canal route and founded the *Institut d'Egypt* for the purpose of historical and scientific research. At this time, his engineers explored the Great Pyramid, uncovering much valuable information. They discovered the corner sockets, peculiar to the Great Pyramid, the relationship of the pyramid's structure and dimensions to astronomical science, and the Rosetta Stone, the key which broke the hieroglyphic code. In August 1799, after distressing news from home, he placed General Kleber in charge and set sail for France.

Napoleon was an enigma to his officers, arising each day to more often than not dispose of pre-existing orders with new ones. His officers were loyal, but exasperated having to frequently frustrate the execution of previous orders with changed commands. Napoleon's second in command, General Kleber, vented his frustrations upon the pages of a personal notebook leaving a record of his thoughts and feelings.

Napoleon apparently relied upon his instincts, accepting the counsel of his staff when it coincided with and elaborated upon his own intuition. It is no surprise then, aware of the discontent within his ranks, he would have kept a document of importance such as the *Book of Fate* in the unfamiliar script of the German language making easy accessibility of its contents difficult, if not impossible, to officers, attendants, or possibly the enemy English.

The order of timing when the oracle was actually received by Napoleon is confused. In the original text, Kirchenhoffer states that the 'Original Egyptian Manuscript (was) Found in the Year 1801, by M. Sonnini in One of the Royal Tombs Near Mount Libycus, in Upper Egypt'. Napoleon left Egypt incognito to return to France in August 1799, therefore — if the dates are correct — Napoleon would not have been able to utilize the oracle upon Egyptian soil. Records show there was a prominent naturalist and traveller named Charles Nicholas Sigisbert Sonnini De Manocourt (1751-1812), renowned for his extensive travels and discoveries.

That Napoleon was predisposed to the use of the oracle is borne out by historical record. This discrepancy in the original text remains a mystery to be revealed perhaps in the future.

As the text from the 1822 edition indicates, the oracle is a translated rendition taken from the papyrus scroll upon which it was originally scribed in hieroglyphics and deposited under the armpit of a mummy of important merit, entrusted with its ancient knowledge, and entitled *The Written Roll of Man's Fate.*

It is believed the *Book of Fate* was dictated to Balaspis, a high priest, by Hermes Trismegistus, the Thrice Great or Thoth, the one gone down through the ages as the 'Messenger of the Gods'. Hermes was called the 'Thrice Greatest' because he was considered the greatest of all philosophers, the greatest of all priests, and the greatest of all kings. It was Hermes who changed the calendar from 360 to 365 days, and is believed to have schooled his wise men in the knowledge of mathematics, medicine, anatomy, astrology, chemistry, law, music, philosophy, geography, oratory, and rhetoric. Eventually, the Greek and Latin worlds revered him as Mercury, the planet nearest the sun, privy to the knowledge of the solar deity and therefore the winged messenger who bestows knowledge of the gods to mortal men upon earth.

Hermes has been credited by Manetho, an Egyptian priest, as the author of 36,000 books, an incredible task by any but the divine. Francis Barrett, in *Biographia Antiqua*, said of Hermes, 'If ever God appeared in man, he appeared in him, as is evident both from his books and his Pymander; in which works he has communicated the sum of the Abyss and the divine knowledge to all posterity'. Madame Blavatsky in her *Secret Doctrine* says, 'Hermes, or rather Thot, was a generic name. Abul Teda shows in *Historia Anti-Islamitica* five Hermes, and the names of Hermes, Nebo, Thot were given respectively in various countries to great initiates'. The deity Thoth, symbolized by the body of a man and the head of an ibis is often used to depict Hermes, and the ibis-headed Thoth is also pictured as a scribe with the crescent shape of the Moon. Historical data concerning Hermes locate him anywhere from circa 11,000 BC to 2,000 BC at the beginning of the decline of the great Egyptian culture.

Historians appear to agree that of the books attributed to Hermes, 42 used in the Egyptian ceremonial processions were housed in the great library at Alexandria. It is believed some volumes escaped the fire and were buried in the desert, their location known only to initiates of the secret schools, secret schools that in our era appear to be discarding the veil of secrecy perhaps due to a dwindling population of the profane having neither the ears to hear nor eyes to see divine wisdom. It is fascinating to see ancient wisdom recycling and emerging through the Piscean mists of secrecy into the Aquarian thirst for consciousness and knowledge. Edgar Cayce, the sleeping prophet of our century, prophesied in one of his trances that the inscribed golden tablets interpreted by Hermes will be discovered in the sands of Egypt before the end of the century.

One of the best works extant today of the writings of Hermes is contained in *The Divine Pymander of Hermes* (translated from the Arabic by Dr Everard in 1650) from a 1978 photographic reproduction by Wizards Bookshelf. The introduction has this to say concerning the 42 books of Hermes:

> 'According to Manetho, this second Hermes or Mercury translated from engraved tablets of stone, that had been hidden in the earth, the sacred characters written by the first Hermes or Mercury, called Thaut or Thoth, and wrote the explanation in books, which were deposited in the Egyptian temples. He thus established a Divine authority, obtained a high degree of respect among the people, and was long revered as the restorer of learning. From the tables of the first Hermes he is said to have written, as commentaries and explanations, an incredible number of books. These books, according to Clemens Alexandrius . . . amounted in number to forty-two. It was impossible for the Egyptians to carry their veneration for them higher than they did. They were borne in their processions with great ceremony and respect. First of all appeared the "Chanter", who had two of them in his hands, one containing the hymns in honour of the gods, and the other rules according to which the kings were to govern. Next came the "Horoscopus", or that minister, as Clemens informs, who carried the four books of astronomy: one treating of the fixed stars, another of the eclipses of the sun and moon, and two last of the rising of these two luminaries. Then appeared the sacred "scribe", with the ten books that treated of cosmography, geography, the description of the nile, etc. Then followed the "stolist", with ten other books, which were names sacerdotal, and treated of the laws of the gods, and of ecclesiastical discipline. "Thus", says the author now cited, "there were forty-two books in all, of which thirty-six comprehended all that belong to the Egyptian philosophy. The other six books regarded medicine, and treated of anatomy, medicaments, diseases of the eyes, of women, and of regulations to be practised in domestic association." '

Hargrave Jennings wrote in the introduction to *The Divine Pymander of Hermes*, 'In a treatise attributed to Albertus Magnus, we are told that the tomb of Hermes was discovered by Alexander the Great in a cave near Hebron. In this was found a slab of emerald . . . and which had inscribed upon it, in Phoenician characters, the precept of the great master concerning the art of making gold. The inscription consisted of thirteen sentences, and is to be found in numerous alchemical works'. Hermes is considered the father of alchemy and his name is mentioned frequently by Zosimos, third century alchemist from Panopoly. Other authorities have said that Isarim, an Initiate, found the emerald slab 'on the dead body of Hermes' at Hebron.

The second statement of the Smaragdine tablet, or the Emerald Table, says 'Secondly — what is below, is like that which is above; and what is above, is like that which is below: to accomplish the miracle of one thing'. You might recognize it in its popular form: *As Above, So Below.* Jennings spoke of the difficulty of interpreting the meaning of the statements but Madame H. P. Blavatsky had no trouble in divining the meaning; '. . . the Tabula Smaragdina of Hermes, the esoteric meaning . . . has seven keys to it. The "One thing" mentioned in it is man. It is said: "The Father of *That One Only Thing* is the Sun; its Mother the Moon; the Wind carries it in his bosom, and its nurse is the Spirituous Earth" '.

This statement has been the foundation upon which astrology bases itself. There is no other way to tell anyone how and why astrology works. It works because the law of time and space is the law humanity must obey and is but a reflection of that which *is*. Every moment — and therefore man as well as all life — contains within itself the blueprint for physical, mental, and spiritual expression which exists at the moment of birth. You could say, man is like a moment in time which got up on two legs and expressed that moment in time for the rest of his life, bumping into harmonious and inharmonious other moments in time through its journey of life. The cosmos, the planets, and the zodiac are eternal scribes for what *is*.

In the Pymander, Hermes receives a divine vision which forms the basis of the knowledge and wisdom, scribed upon tablets for humanity. Here are some selected verses from Book Two:

> 12. But whence . . . are the Elements of Nature made? Of the Will and counsel of God; which taking the Word, and beholding the beautiful

World (in the Archetype thereof) imitated it, and so made this World, by the principles and vital seed or Soul-like productions of itself.

13. For the Mind being God, Male and Female, Life and Light, brought forth by his Word another Mind or Workman; which being God of the Fire, and the Spirit, fashioned and formed seven other Governors, which in the circles contain the Sensible World, whose Government or disposition is called *Fate* or *Destiny*.

15. But the Workman, Mind, together with the Word, containing the circles, and whirling them about, turned round as a wheel, his own Workmanships; and suffered them to be turned from an indefinite Beginning to an indeterminable end, for they always begin where they end.

18. But the Father of all things, the Mind being Life and Light, brought forth Man like unto himself, whom he loved as his proper Birth; for he was all beauteous, having the image of his Father.

26. And from this cause Man above all things that live upon earth is double: Mortal, because of his body, and Immortal, because of the substantial Man. For being immortal, and having power of all things, he yet suffers mortal things, and such as are subject to *Fate* or *Destiny*.

The vision speaks of the mystery of man concealed in the nature of matter, within the infinite circle of beginning and ending which endlessly turns as the fates and destinies of men are played out, governed by the seven governors (the seven sacred planets within the body — the seven chakras), created by a deity of duality, male and female in its own likeness.

The vision imparted much of the same knowledge Christian mystics have related through the past Piscean era. In verse 40, the Pymander cautions 'But he that thro' the error of Love loved the Body, abideth wandering in darkness, sensible, suffering the things of death'. The darkness represented the separation from 'Light and Life' of the Mind which created man. The Pymander, like the Bible, indicates the Light is within, whereby making a search for fulfilment in the world of matter a serious detour toward the realm of darkness, pain, and misery. 'The light shineth in darkness and the darkness comprehended it not.' John 1:5.

Man finds himself in the dilemma of straddling two realms — spirit and matter. Born of matter in a material existence yet also born of a divine creator, he ever must recognize the divine operating through all creation, however painful or pleasant the role in which he finds himself cast. He must follow the example of the Hansa, a fabulous bird which, as every Hindu knows, when given milk mixed with water for its food, separates the two, drinking the milk and leaving the water, showing wisdom (milk symbolizing spirit and water representing matter).

The issue of fate vs. free will has been debated for aeons and the argument appears no closer to settlement today. Current thought on the issue among New Age thinkers appears to favour free will. The great Swiss psychoanalyst, Carl Gustav Jung, concluded toward the end of years of study and research on the psyche of man that 'free will is the ability to do gladly that which I must do', thereby implying Fate is having to do it anyway.

Astrologer Margaret Hone appears to have agreed with Jung when she wrote, 'Only by the recognition of that which he [man] senses as greater than himself can he attune himself to what is beyond the terrestrial pattern, though he may not escape terrestrial happenings, by . . . free and willing "acceptance" he can "will" his real self free in its reaction to them'. St Thomas Aquinas, mystic, scholar/teacher and astrologer, said 'I am convinced that every man derives his will power from a planetary sphere of influence which he uses or abuses . . . hence astrology teaches that character is *Destiny*, and also that the wise man rules his stars, while the fool obeys them'.

Knowledge and awareness bring one to wisdom, as ignorance leads to insensibility. St Catherine of Siena said, 'The soul yearning desire for the honour of God . . . begins by remaining in the cell of self-knowledge in order to know better the goodness of God.'

In alchemy, the *Great Work* is man himself. Stated quite simply and relating to the great esoteric teachings throughout the ages, man learns to recognize his inherent divinity within his daily trudging throughout life, transforming the leaden basis of earthly existence into the spiritual gold of divine Light, changing him from the leaden man into the anthropos, or heavenly man.

In alchemical tradition, to accomplish the *work*, a union or a conjunction of the opposites is necessary; the higher with the lower, spirit and matter, beautiful and ugly, hot and cold, and so on. An in-depth analysis of Jung's study of the 'Seven Sermons of the Dead' by Basilides of Alexandria, 'the city where East and West meet' can be found in Stephan A. Hoeller's *The Gnostic Jung and the Seven Sermons of the Dead*. Abraxas, 'a rooster-headed god with serpent feet, in whom light and darkness are both united and transcended' is a mythological symbol adopted by gnostic and alchemical traditions. The dead to whom the sermons are delivered to is common humanity who are asleep or dead to the truths of the sermons being given.

The seven sermons are similar to the books of Pymander, and rich with esoteric meaning. It is within the daily cycles that we take for granted that deeper truths are hidden, and in the ordinariness of life can be found the hidden gold. As Dr Hoeller says, the alchemical processes are simply '. . . the conjunction of what is out there and what comes forth in response to what is out there from within'.

The *Book of Fate*, published as the Oracle of Napoleon Bonaparte, concerns the queries of everyday life. It is a part of our wholeness to address the issue of daily life if we are to really participate in the *Great Work*. Whether Napoleon fulfilled his destiny with any more or less consciousness or awareness we may never know, but it is my conclusion as an astrologer who addresses the concerns of daily life with my clientèle on many levels, that gaining clarity on any question provides the querent with the wisdom to rule his stars and the free will to gladly do that which he must do anyway.

As I was pondering upon whether to edit and resurrect the *Book of Fate*, I cracked open a 'fortune cookie' at a Chinese restaurant and read, 'It is never wrong to ask a question. It is always wrong to be ignorant'.

BONNIE PARKER

The Book of Fate

The following text is a reproduction of the original *Book of Fate*. The questions and the answers of the original text have been revised to accommodate current language usage. The content and the meaning of the original questions and answers have not been altered and suitable synonyms have been selected in preference of archaic words. Likewise, some of the symbols current in England in 1822 have been updated to reflect symbols in use today with the Egyptian motif.

THE

BOOK OF FATE,

FORMERLY IN THE POSSESSION

OF

NAPOLEON,

LATE

EMPEROR OF FRANCE;

AND

NOW FIRST RENDERED INTO ENGLISH,

FROM A

German Translation,

OF AN

ANCIENT EGYPTIAN MANUSCRIPT,

FOUND IN THE YEAR 1801, BY M. SONNINI,

IN ONE OF THE

ROYAL TOMBS,

NEAR MOUNT LIBYCUS, IN UPPER EGYPT.

BY H. KIRCHENHOFFER,
FELLOW OF THE UNIVERSITY OF PAVIA;
KNIGHT GRAND CROSS OF THE ANNUNCIADE OF
SARDINIA; AND CHEVALIER OF THE LEGION OF
HONOUR

LONDON
1822.

Dedication

TO HER IMPERIAL HIGHNESS

MARIE LOUISE,

EX-EMPRESS OF FRANCE, ARCH-DUCHESS OF PARMA, &c. &c.

MADAM,

IT is with feelings of the most devout respect and veneration, that, by your Imperial permission, I take the present opportunity of laying the following Work at your Highness's feet.

According to your Imperial Highness's gracious commands, this Translation, although in some passages free, (in order to adapt it to the customs of England,) is still almost a *fac-simile* of the only and original Manuscript, lately in possession of the ever-to-be-lamented Emperor and King.

In adhering strictly to your Imperial commands, I hope that my endeavours to embellish the Work, according to the original Drawings, will meet with your Imperial Highness's gracious approbation.

With feelings of the most profound Respect,

I remain, Your Imperial Highness's Devoted Servant,

HERMAN KIRCHENHOFFER.

London, 1st June, 1822.

Translator's Preface

The following Work is translated from a Manuscript in the German language, which was found among the camp equipage belonging to the late Emperor of France, when he retreated from Leipzic, after the defeat of his army, in the year 1813. It fell to the lot of a Prussian officer, who, ignorant of its value, sold it for a few Napoleons to a French general officer, then a prisoner of war in the fortress of Köningsburg. This gentleman aware of its great importance, and knowing from Napoleon's arms, which were emblazoned upon it, that it once belonged to his imperial master, was resolved on his return to France to present it at the Tuilleries; but, alas! he did not live to accomplish this purpose; for, although his medical attendants gave him every hope of recovery from his wounds, their efforts to restore him to health proved unavailing, for he died soon after from mortification which took place after amputation of the right arm.

By will, hastily drawn up, the personal effects of this officer were transmitted to his family, who were enjoined to take the earliest opportunity of putting the Manuscript in question into the Emperor's own hands; but Napoleon's manifold occupations, both civil and military, from time to time, prevented this.

During the early part of Napoleon's ostracism in St Helena, means were found of conveying the Manuscript to the Empress, who unfortunately never had an opportunity, although she eagerly sought for it, of sending it to her husband. After his death her Highness gave the Translator her imperial permission for its publication in the English language.

Regarding the purpose which Napoleon had in view in the private perusal of this Work, it is necessary to inform the Reader; but, previous to this, it will be proper to state the manner in which he himself became possessed of it.

It is well known that, in 1801, many French artists and literati accompanied the First Consul in his famous expedition to Egypt, for the purpose of exploring the antiquities of that celebrated region, where once flourished the arts and sciences, in greater perfection than in any other country in the world, the most civilized nations of Europe in the present day, not excepted. At the head of the 'Commission of Arts' was M. Sonnini, whose travels have since excited so much attention. This gentleman having succeeded in perforating a passage into the interior chamber of one of the royal tombs in Mount Libycus, near Thebes, found therein a sarcophagus, in which was a mummy of extraordinary beauty, and in fine preservation. Having examined this curiosity very minutely, he discovered, attached by a peculiar kind of gum to the left breast, a long roll of papyrus, which, having unrolled, greatly excited his curiosity on account of the hieroglyphics which were beautifully painted on it.

M. Sonnini's description of these tombs, which are of the most astonishing structure, is as follows: 'The whole of the mountain Libycus, which begins at half a league to the west of the Memnonium, and ends immediately opposite to Medinet-abou, is pierced from its base to three-fourths of its elevation with a great number of sepulchral grottos. Those which are nearest the surface of the ground are the most spacious, as well as the most decorated; those which are in the most elevated part of the mountain are much more rudely contrived and executed; while such as hold the middle place, bear an adjusted proportion of space and ornament. Those which belong to the poor are the most interesting, because they always contain some representation of the arts which flourished, and the trades which were practised, at that epocha. The plan of these grottos is in a great measure the same. A door, opening towards the east, displays a gallery of about 20 feet in length, which is sometimes formed in a straight line, and at other times runs off from the entrance in a right angle: it is indifferently supported by columns or pilasters, of which the number varies from four to ten. At the extremity of the gallery are wells which lead to the catacombs, where the mummies are deposited. The depth of these wells varies from 40 to 60 feet, and they are connected with long subterraneous passages, rudely shaped in the rock, which terminate in a chamber of about 30 feet square, whose sides are supported by pilasters, and contain large remains of the mummies. There are evident traces of numerous other subterraneous communications, which probably lead to other chambers, that are at present concealed.

'In the upper gallery are sculptured in basso-relievo, or painted in fresco, a crowd of subjects relating to funeral ceremonies. The most interesting pictures which are seen there, offer a detail of circumstances connected with the ancient inhabitants of the country. There, are represented their first occupations, such as the chase and the fishery; thence we may trace the progress of civilization, in the employments of the sadler, the cartwright, the potter, the money-changer, the husbandman, and in the duties and punishments of military life. Each grotto is adorned with a ceiling painted with subjects of fancy, and whose design is exactly the same as that of the paper-hangings which were fashionable in France about thirty years ago.

'The tombs of the kings are about 6,400 paces from the river. They have been formed in a narrow valley, in the centre of the mountain Libycus. The ancient way thither is not known, and the spot is now gained by an artificial passage. These sepulchres occupy a large ravine, which is flanked by the bed of a torrent. The plan of one of these tombs will be sufficient to explain the general disposition of the rest. Every grotto communicates with the valley by a large gate, which opens to a gallery hollowed in the rock: its breadth and height are generally about 12 feet, and its length is 20 paces to the second gate, which opens to another gallery of the same breadth, and 24 feet in length. To the right and left of this gallery are chambers of five feet in breadth and ten feet long. There, are found paintings of arms such as hatchets, poignards, curvated sabres, straight swords, lances, javelins, bows, arrows, quivers, coats of mail, shields, implements of husbandry, vases, and trinkets of every kind. The detail of preparing food is also represented.

'A third gallery succeeds, of the same dimensions as the former, and leads to a chamber above the level of the other apartments, which is 18 feet square. This chamber is the entrance to a gallery of 34 paces in length; there is also an inclining gallery, whose length is 28 paces. At its extremity is a corridor of 16 paces, leading to a chamber of 11 paces square, which is connected with another of the same size by a gallery of six paces. A square saloon then succeeds, supported by eight pillars; its length is 20 paces, and its breadth 20. Here is the sarcophagus which contained the mummy of the king. The Romans made some attempts to carry away this sarcophagus from the grotto where it is deposited; they had even tried to level the ground, in order to facilitate its removal, but they very soon renounced the impracticable enterprise.

'To the saloon of the sarcophagus, another apartment succeeds, of 25 paces in breadth, and 40 in length. The height of the tomb is seven feet, its length eight, and its breadth six: the total length of the gallery is 225 paces. The tombs of the kings throughout their whole extent are covered with pictures and hieroglyphics;* but the greater part are painted in fresco, and represent the most fantastic subjects that can be conceived. Here it was that the Romans caught that idea of the grotesque, which formed a principal subject of their compositions during the second and third ages of the empire. The researches

* The Egyptian priests, to keep the mysteries of their religion from the knowledge of the common people, used Hieroglyphics, or sacred characters, as the word itself imports, being a Greek compound, signifying 'sacred' and 'to engrave or carve'.

into Herculaneum have discovered a great number of paintings executed in a similar taste.

'One of the most interesting of these grottos contains a sarcophagus that is still entire and in its place. Its length is 16 feet, its height 12, and its breadth six. It still preserves the lid, adorned with the effigy of the king, which is a single block of granite. The astonishment that is felt, on reflecting that this enormous mass was transported to the extremity of a subterraneous passage 200 paces in length, exceeds all bounds, when it is considered that it was worked upon the place where it remains. What difficulties must have been surmounted, in order to transport a weight of many hundred miliers, across the almost impracticable roads of the mountain! Here it was that we found the famous mummy and papyrus roll.

'Human sacrifices are continually represented, as well as a diversity of curious heiroglyphical figures, one of which represents Isis walking on the Earth, and flowers springing forth from under her feet.

'From the time of Strabo, there were reckoned 17 tombs of kings: and we shall still find the same number, if we may comprehend in this enumeration a superb grotto, whose plan is equally large and beautiful with that of the sepulchres of the Theban sovereigns. This grotto is half a league to the north of the Memnonium, and is scooped out at the bottom of a mountain, whose inclosures contain many other tombs: the entrance of several of them is closed, and the greater part of them have been violated. It appears that those of the ancient Egyptians who had remained faithful to their worship, endeavoured, from respect to the memory of their princes, to conceal the knowledge of their sepulchres, either from their conquerors or the professors of other religions.

'The ancient Egyptians, from the king to the lowest of his subjects, were very attentive to the construction of their burying-places, in the firm belief that, after several thousand years, the soul would return to inhabit the body, if, during that time, it should have remained undisturbed. Hence proceeded the custom of embalming, and the position of sepulchres in places inaccessible to the inundation of the river.

'In the neighbourhood of the Memnonium, and among the grottos of private individuals, many are found which are still filled with the fragments of mummies. When the Arabs, who consider the grottos as the property of each family, apprehend that they may be visited by strangers, they set fire to the mummies which they contain, in order to turn the curious from the research. There are some of these caverns still untouched; as the persevering traveller has not yet discovered them.

'The sepulchres of the rich are exhausted. None of the mummies which are sold by the people of the country are dressed in the envelope, upon which the figure of *Death* was painted. A few fragments of these envelopes are all which now appear. It is indeed very extraordinary that, except in the present instance, no traveller has found the manuscripts on the papyrus, which the mummies of distinguished persons never fail to enclose. These manuscripts are, without contradiction, the most ancient that have been preserved, and appear to contain the prayers made for the dead, and also the mysterious books used by the priests. They are written in hieroglyphics or characters, and are decorated with drawings that resemble the pictures which cover the walls of the sepulchres. Many of the mummies have the nails, both of their hands and feet, gilt. Two rolls of the papyrus are sometimes found with them, which are often placed under the armpits, though they are also deposited in the division of the thighs, and near the organs of generation.'

M. Sonnini hastened to the First Consul, whose curiosity, likewise, being much excited by viewing this hieroglyphical treasure, sent for a learned Copt, who, after an attentive perusal, discovered a key whereby he was enabled to decypher the characters. After great labour, he accomplished this task, and dictated its contents to Napoleon's secretary who, in order to preserve the matter secret, translated and wrote them down in the German language.

The First Consul, having consulted the German translation of the roll regarding some transactions in his own life, was amazed to find that the answers given corresponded strictly with what had actually occurred. He accordingly secured the original and translated Manuscripts in his private cabinet, which ever after accompanied him, until the fatal day of Leipzic above mentioned. They were held by him as a sacred treasure, and are said to have been a stimulus to many of his grandest speculations, he being known to consult them on all occasions. Before each campaign, and on the eve of every battle or treaty, Napoleon consulted his favourite Oracle. His grief for the loss of this companion of his private hours was excessive; and it is said that, at Leipzic, he even ran the risk of being taken, in his eagerness to preserve the cabinet containing it from destruction.

In a list, drawn up in Napoleon's own handwriting, on a blank leaf prefixed to the translated Manuscript, are to be seen the following Questions, as put to the Oracle, with their Answers, as received by that illustrious man. They are here selected, from among many others, on account of the very strong analogy, I might say identity, which exists between them and some of the most important actions of his life.

Question 15. *What is the aspect of the seasons, and what political changes are likely to take place?*

Answer. (*Hieroglyphic of Cross Keys*) 'A conqueror, of noble mind and mighty power, shall spring from low condition; he will break the chains of the oppressed, and will give liberty to the nations.'

Question 12. *Will my name be immortalized, and will posterity applaud it?*
Answer. (*Hieroglyphic of Pyramid*) 'Thy name will be handed down, with the memory of thy deeds, to the most distant posterity.

Question 8. *Shall I be eminent, and meet with preferment in my pursuits?*
Answer. (*Hieroglyphic of Pyramid*) 'Thou shalt meet with many obstacles, but at length thou shalt attain the highest earthly power and honour.'

Question 12. *Will my name be immortalized, and will posterity applaud it?*
Answer. (*Hieroglyphic of Castle*) 'Abuse not the power which the Lord giveth thee, and thy name will be hailed with rapture in future ages.'

Question 30. *Have I any, or many, enemies?*
Answer. (*Hieroglyphic of Hand and Dagger*) 'Thou hast enemies who, if not restrained by the laws, would plunge a dagger in thy heart.'

Question 15. *What is the aspect of the seasons, and what political changes are likely to take place?*
Answer. (*Hieroglyphic of Castle*) 'The wings of the eagle of the north will be clipped, and his talons blunted.'

I shall forbear further quotation, as the rest of the answers in the list are either obscure or relative to matters of inferior or domestic import.

Regarding the personal application of the above answers (except the last, of which I shall speak presently,) to the late Emperor, there can be no difference of opinion: this is too obvious to admit of a moment's discussion; indeed, I have been confidently informed, that when he aspired to the imperial throne, he was actually transported with rapture and amazement, when he read the words contained in the answer to question 8: 'Thou shalt meet with many obstacles, but at length thou shalt attain the highest earthly power and honour.'

In the second answer to question 15, that is, the last which I have quoted from the Emperor's list, the reader will perceive that the Autocrat of Russia is indicated; but whether the words have any direct reference to what passed before the treaty of Tilsit, or to any future boundaries which have been, or may be, opposed to Russian aggrandizement, is not equally certain. At all events, it must be allowed, that Napoleon's invasion of Russian territory clearly proves that his own sentiments were in entire accordance with the latter suggestion.

It had been a happy circumstance for Napoleon, had he uniformly abided, or been ruled by answers to many other questions, which he was in the habit of putting to the Oracle, and which, doubtless, forewarned him of danger, and, most probably, of his downfall: but he was so accustomed, from a long series of success in almost every pursuit which he undertook, to look on the bright side of every circumstance, that, to a mind like his, such forewarnings were not likely to be productive of that salutary restraint which some of his speculations required.

As instances of the lamentable effects of this want of confidence in the Oracular counsels contained in the following Work, I may adduce the battle of Leipzic itself, and the fatal consequences of the Russian campaign, *viz.* the conflagration of Moscow, the destruction of his brave army, and, finally, the abdication of a sceptre which he was long accustomed to wave over the heads of those very monarchs who now compelled him to relinquish it.

To return to the subject of the Manuscripts themselves: What became of the original Papyrus is not known, but it is supposed that from the frailness of its texture, it was destroyed in the general pillage. If, however, it should be in existence, the present proprietor is hereby earnestly entreated to communicate thereupon with the Secretary of Her Imperial Highness, making whatever demand for its restoration which he may deem requisite; or he may, if more convenient, deposit it in the Imperial Museum at Vienna, where he shall obtain a receipt for the same in due form. In the care of the administrators of the Museum, he is required to leave a sealed letter, addressed to Her Imperial Highness's Secretary, containing the demand of money, which he feels himself entitled to, in the way of remuneration.

It remains now for the Translator to say something respecting the nature and quality of the Answers which are contained in the *Book of Fate*. In the first place, then, respecting the nature of the Answers, it will appear that some of these seem to have so direct a reference to the manners and customs of the present age, as almost to deprive them of the same just claims to antiquity which it will be allowed the others undoubtedly possess. But this impression will speedily vanish, when we call to mind that among the ancient Egyptians the same arts were cultivated as are now carried on in England and other countries at the present day. Do not the paintings in the tombs, which are still in preservation in Egypt, prove this? It is likewise necessary to take into account that the work has already passed through two successive translations, consequently, in some passages there must be a considerable deterioration from the original sense; but more particularly, as in phrases of a domestic or professional application, it is sometimes impossible to preserve the real idiom of a translated language.

In my own case, I have to state, that from a long residence in this country, I have been enabled to attain a knowledge of many of the peculiarities both of customs and language among the English people. This knowledge has been of great use in my recent labours, and it will account for those slight deviations which I have sometimes found necessary, in adapting an ancient Egyptian work to modern eyes and ears. These deviations, however, are few and, I may add, slight; but they will be more certainly appreciated when the Reader has had an opportunity of perusing the present translation, and then comparing it with the German and French ones, which I intend to have published immediately on my return to the Continent.

In the second place, regarding the *quality* of the Answers, I have to observe, that they are of five kinds: *positive*, *mandatory*, *presumptive*, *admonitory* and *conditional*. As examples, I shall select five (that is, one of each quality) from among 17, which have been returned to various persons who consulted the Oracle since it has been in my possession.

First, then, of the *positive*. It was asked (*question 17*), by a gentleman, 'Will my beloved prove true in my absence?' The Answer returned was (*Hieroglyphic of the Plough*), 'The affections of the being whom thou lovest, will be placed on none other but thyself'.

Example of the *mandatory*. It was asked (*question 6*), 'Shall I make, or mar, my fortune by gambling?' The answer was (*Hieroglyphic of Cross Bones*), 'Be warned! from henceforth, never play for money, nor money's worth'.

As an example of the *presumptive*, it was asked (*question 28*), 'Shall I ever find a treasure?'. The answer was such as to leave no doubt on the consulter's mind that he should find a treasure; but at the same time it contained such good counsel, as to the application of it, as was absolutely required by a man of his circumstances and disposition. It was (*Hieroglyphic of Fasces*), 'When thou findest a treasure, teach thy tongue to be silent, and see that thou makest good use of thy riches'.

To exemplify the *admonitory*, I may give an instance of a lady who consulted the Oracle in the following words (*question 24*), 'Inform me of all particulars relating to my future husband'. The answer was (*Hieroglyphic of the Bow and Arrow*), 'Consider well whether thou oughtest, at present, to change thy condition in life'.

Lastly, as an example of the *conditional* answers, I select the following. It was asked (*question 19*), by the mother of a large family, 'After my death will my children be virtuous and happy?' The answer was (*Hieroglyphic of the Ladder*), 'In the training of thy offspring, let thy discipline be strict, but not severe; lose no opportunity of improving their understandings, and, in the plenitude of their happiness, they will bless thee'.

Another quality which pertains to a few of these answers is the close affinity which seems to exist between them and some of the most favourite moral axioms in use among the civilized nations of antiquity: but is this to be wondered at, when we consider that Egypt had long been the residence of the Hebrews, and that it had been overrun both by the Greeks and Romans, who afterwards formed settlements there? It cannot be doubted, therefore, that the Hebrews not only retained the arts which they saw cultivated, and learned, in Egypt, but also that their priests became possessors of copies of books which were in use in the temples. That the Greeks and Romans did so, is beyond speculation; for it is well known (being asserted by Herodotus and other historians) that all the Oracles, afterwards established in the states of Greece, and elsewhere, owed their origin to books found in the Egyptian temples, which were pillaged and plundered upwards of 3000 years ago. That these books were mere transcripts of the original copy of the work now given to the world, there can likewise be no doubt; consequently, the inference is a fair one, that, the moral axioms, above spoken of, were borrowed from these books, and that, being greatly admired by the literati of those days, such passages were afterwards transplanted into their own works as original.

This explanation of the apparent identity will be perfectly satisfactory to every candid reader; but in order to throw as much light on the subject as possible, I have prefixed to the present work an authentic and interesting account of the *Oracles* which bore so famous a part in the histories of ancient Egypt and Greece.

The Translator, in taking his leave of the British public, has now merely to state that the *Book of Fate*, in its English dress, is adapted to all conditions of life; and persons of every rank and capacity will now have an opportunity of consulting it, and of regulating their future conduct according to its Oracular counsels.

H. KIRCHENHOFFER

June 1822

The Writing of Balaspis
By Command of Hermes Trismegistus Unto the Priests of the Great Temple

Priests of Thebais! Servants in the great temple of Hecatompylos! Ye who in the sacred city of Diospolis have dedicated your lives to the service of the King of the Gods and of men! Hermes,* the interpreter of the will of Osiris, greets you!

It is the will of the Gods, in grand assembly convened, that ye preserve your lives free from stain and pollution.

It is their will that ye continue to instruct the nations, as far as they may be permitted to know.

It is the pleasure of Osiris, sitting on his throne of clouds, and surrounded by the inferior deities, that ye make known to his subjects, his children upon earth, whatever may concern their *Destiny*, and what matters ye shall find written in the book of books — *The Written Roll of Man's Fate*, now committed to your safe keeping — that ye do this strictly and truly, without fear of danger or hope of reward, according to all questions that may be asked, by individual persons, by tribes, by rulers of states, and by conquerors of nations.

Osiris commandeth the servants in his favoured sanctuary to show favour unto none, in the answers which it will be their duty to give from this book.

* To Hermes Trismegistus, a sage as highly revered among them as Zoroaster was among the Persians, the Egyptians ascribed the inventions of chief use to human life; and like every people who are unable to settle the antiquity of their origin, they represented his works to have outstood the shock even of the universal deluge. They otherwise called him Thoth, and their priests constantly maintained that from the hieroglyphical characters upon the pillars he erected, and the sacred books, all the philosophy and learning of the world has been derived, and all the Oracular intelligence has been drawn.

Let sacrifices and gifts and invocations be made; let the question be asked in all humility and strong faith, and when the Diviner hath consulted the windings and intricacies of the problem, according to the instructions hereunto appended, let the result be written and handed to the chief Prophet or Prophetess (seated on a stool having three legs) who shall read and interpret the writing of Hermes unto the enquirer, in the face of all the assembled people.

And the Prophet or Prophetess shall read no writing but what hath been truly given to her by the priest who doth officiate in the sacrifice; and the priest shall not add to, nor diminish from, what he findeth to be the true answer to the question asked, as in this *Roll of Man's Fate* contained: neither shall he substitute one answer for another, but in all things he shall do according to the instructions herein given.

The highest among the Gods, in like way, ordaineth that no bribe nor private gift shall be offered or taken, either by the individual who enquireth or by the priest who maketh answer to the consultation: let the gift, which is to be offered, be of free will, and let it be put upon the altar after the sacrifice hath been consumed, in the face of all the people. If herein the priests offend, they shall, on the instant, be struck down and pinioned to the earth by the piercing and fiery arrows which the great Osiris in his anger, speaking from the clouds, hurleth at offending mortals. Look to it that in this ye offend not.

It is further enjoined that ye take strict charge of this book; that no one but the priests do touch it with their hands, and that it be preserved in a chest of alabaster, to be placed under the altar in the midst of the temple. It is in like way commanded that copies of the book be written as occasion requireth, and that they be transmitted unto the priests of the other temples throughout the earth: also that they be deposited in the tombs of the Kings and of the High Priests, as followeth:

When the body hath been embalmed and sufficiently swathed in fine cloth, let the roll of writing be placed under the left breast, and let the vestment be bound over it, so that it shall be covered close and hid from view. The body shall then be attended by the princes and priests and people to the place of sepulture, where it is to be interred with honour — a strong and durable building being raised on the top thereof.

How the Enquirer Shall Obtain a True Answer to the Question Which He Putteth to the Oracle

When a man or woman doth come to enquire ought of you, oh priests, let the gifts be made and the sacrifices offered up, and let the invocations of the servants of the temple be chanted.

When silence hath been restored, the Diviner shall direct the stranger who hath come to enquire of the Oracle, to trace, with a reed dipped in the blood

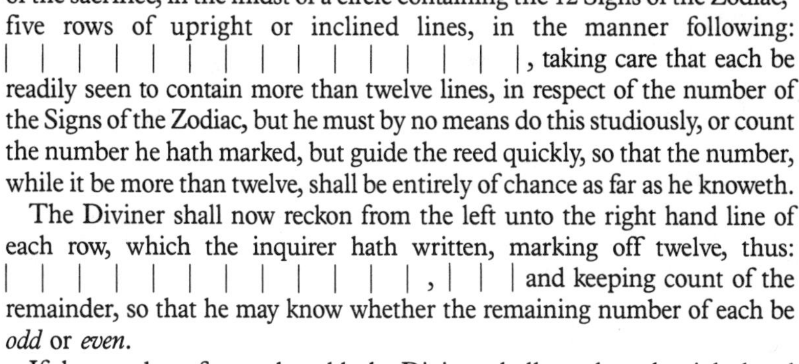

of the sacrifice, in the midst of a circle containing the 12 Signs of the Zodiac,* five rows of upright or inclined lines, in the manner following: | | | | | | | | | | | | | | |, taking care that each be readily seen to contain more than twelve lines, in respect of the number of the Signs of the Zodiac, but he must by no means do this studiously, or count the number he hath marked, but guide the reed quickly, so that the number, while it be more than twelve, shall be entirely of chance as far as he knoweth.

The Diviner shall now reckon from the left unto the right hand line of each row, which the inquirer hath written, marking off twelve, thus: | | | | | | | | | | | |, | | | and keeping count of the remainder, so that he may know whether the remaining number of each be *odd* or *even*.

If the number of a row be odd, the Diviner shall attach to the right hand side thereof one small star, and if it be even, he shall attach two stars; and in the same manner with the other rows, as herein set down:

| | | | | | | | | | | |, | | | ★ (odd)
| | | | | | | | | | | |, | | ★ ★ (even)
| | | | | | | | | | | |, | | | | | ★ (odd)
| | | | | | | | | | | |, | | ★ ★ (even)
| | | | | | | | | | | |, | | | | ★ ★ (even)

This double column of stars shall be, to the Diviner, for a Sign whereby he shall be enabled to discover the Fate of the Enquirer.

Let the Enquirer now consult his own breast what he requireth to know; and whether the matter cometh within compass of the questions herein writ, and set down in order, as followeth.† If it doth, the Enquirer shall straightway pronounce the question, audibly, as it is written, without adding to, or diminishing therefrom, and shall, while he uttereth the words, point to the number of the question with the forefinger of his *left* hand.

* The Translator feels it incumbent on him here to notice (from the experience of himself and others in consulting the Oracle) that he considers some of the above mentioned formalities may, on most occasions, be dispensed with. He has found that for all *ordinary* consultations the circle and signs may be omitted; and instead of a reed dipped in blood, he and his friends have, invariably and without the least detriment, used a *pen* dipped in *common ink*. As to the gifts, sacrifices, and invocations, he considers them in a Christian land to be entirely superfluous; but in their stead it is doubtless requisite that the consulter should have a firm reliance on the goodness and providence of the Creator of all things.

† See the Appendix containing the questions, their hieroglyphics and signs.

The Diviner, in his proper vestments, having invoked Osiris, shall now place the forefinger of his *right* hand on the spot whereon the Enquirer had previously placed the same finger of his left. He shall then search out among the Signs, or columns of stars, placed above the hieroglyphics, for that *individual* Sign, or column, which shall answer in every respect to the one which hath been cast up, by the addition of the lines previously traced by the Enquirer.

When the Diviner hath found the corresponding Sign, or column of stars, he must place thereon the forefinger of his *left* hand; he shall now move this finger, and likewise the same finger of the right hand, from the points whereon they have been placed, so that they may approximate, or meet each other, at right angles.

The Hieroglyphic whereat the fingers meet, must now be noted; and the Diviner, having looked into the roll, is therein to search out the *counterpart* of the same Hieroglyphic.

Having found it, he is to search further on the left hand side of the matter, or answers, appended unto this Hieroglyphic, for the counterpart of the Sign, or column of stars, which, in the commencement of the consultation, had incidentally, or *by the ordination of Fate*, been produced by the enumeration of the surplus over 12, of the lines traced by the Enquirer within the circle.

The words attached to the Sign, or column of stars, will be the just and true answer to the question put; which see no one do pervert to any false purpose of deceit, enmity or wickedness.

No further ceremony now remaineth, but that the Priest who hath acted in the divination, do write down the answer truly, and, with his finger placed upon his lips, hand it unto the Prophet or Prophetess, who shall in a loud voice proclaim its contents unto the person who came to enquire.*

* In order to make the English reader, as much as possible, acquainted with the proper mode of finding answers to the questions of those who consult the Oracle, it will be necessary here to state one example. I shall take the same rows of lines, and the same Sign, or double column of stars, as are set down in the original instructions for consultation, as above. We shall suppose, then, that the Question asked is no. 27, as marked in the Appendix, viz: *Shall my intended journey be blessed or unfortunate?*

By looking at the column of stars, or Sign, corresponding with that cast up, we shall find it numbered *20*, and the consequent Hieroglyphic produced by the combination of this Sign and the Question asked, will be that of Mars.

Now by reference to this Hieroglyphic and its subservient Sign, or column of stars, in the *Book of Fate* (page 108) we find that the answer given by the Oracle is, 'When thou hast arrived at thy place of destination, lose no time in executing thy errand, and return without delay', which answer, whilst it suggests a necessary caution, whereby evil or danger is avoided, perfectly corresponds with the Question asked.

In a similar way, appropriate answers will be given to all the other Questions in the

In conclusion, I am commanded to write unto you, that it is the duty of the Priests to instruct all those who consult the Oracle that it behoveth them to be contented with whatever answer they may, through Fate, receive; and to follow implicitly, and without reservation, whatever the Oracle, in its answers, may happen to dictate. If the instructions of Hermes be not obeyed, what booteth it to enquire? If the Consulter be herein disobedient to the will of Osiris, the evil be upon his own head.

Further, oh Priests, be warned to make no divination, nor to admit of any gift, sacrifice or consultation, save during the night season, and that, too, only whilst Isis shineth in the fullness of her beauty.* Neither shall ye give answers on those days or nights in which either Osiris who ruleth the heavens by day, or the Queen of his love, who ruleth by night, do veil the comeliness and majesty of their countenances from the eyes of mortals, and whilst they do retire from the labours of their celestial course, within the chambers of their sanctuary of rest.†

These are the words which I, Balaspis, have been commanded, by my great master Hermes Trismegistus, to write unto you, oh Priests of Thebais.

Table; that is, by paying attention to their particular Hieroglyphics and Signs.

N.B. The Translator considers it proper to state, that in order to facilitate the search for the Hieroglyphic (resulting from the combination of the Question and Sign,) in the *Book of Fate*, it will be proper for the Consulter to cast his eye over the Key to the Oracles in the Appendix, and to note the number of the page which lies immediately after the corresponding symbol.

* I presume that here the meaning of Balaspis is that the Oracle should not be consulted but when the Moon is at the full. Among the ancient Egyptians Isis typified the Moon, whilst the name of Osiris was always given to the Sun.

† By this mode of expression, it is evident that eclipses of the Sun and Moon are meant: But it is necessary to notice that, as far as the experience of the Translator and his friends has enabled them to judge, there is no apparent reason or necessity for confining the consultation of the Oracle to any particular time or season. One thing, however, the Consulter should be aware of, is that it would be improper for him to ask *two* questions on the same day; or even to ask the *same* questions, with reference to the same subject, twice within one calendar month.

THE ORACLES

How to Use the Oracle

As Balaspis cautions on page 33 the Diviner or Inquirer is to create five rows or lines and without consciously counting each stroke, make vertical lines as follows: | | | | | | | | | | | | | |.

Once the lines are drawn, go back and count the number of vertical lines in each row, note whether they are numbered odd or even, and to the right of the line place one star if odd, and two stars if even. Make sure each line counts more than 12.* If the number of lines are 12 or less, quickly mark more lines without counting. (You may photocopy the 'Oracle Reading' form at the end of the book for your own use.) For example:

| | | | | | | | | | | | , | | (14 - even) ★★

Once the lines are drawn, counted, and a column of stars created, you must seriously consider and meditate upon the question which resides within. You then find the question from the list of 32 that most closely matches your true question. As Balaspis wrote:

> 'Let the Enquirer now consult his own breast what he requireth to know; and whether the matter cometh within compass of the question herein writ, and set down in order, as followeth. If it doth, the Enquirer shall straightway pronounce the question, audibly, as it is written, without

* The counting of vertical lines past the number 12 represents going beyond the boundaries and limitations of man's universal magistrate, the zodiacal universe, upon which he has been charted to steer his own course. The answers, therefore, come from a realm which extend beyond our own.

adding to, or diminishing therefrom, and shall, while he uttereth the words, point to the number of the question with the forefinger of his *left* hand.'

Find the column of stars from the top of the *Table of Questions and Oracles* (on pages 204-5) and go down that column until it meets the square on the line of your question number (the questions are on pages 202-3). The symbol in that square represents the number of the Oracle that contains your answer. Go to that Oracle. The same column of stars you created within that Oracle is your answer.

For example, a friend used the Oracle to discover whether the health of her mother would improve. The column of stars she built was:

★★
★
★★
★★
★★

She asked Question 25, *Shall the patient recover from illness?* which most closely resembled her personal question, 'Will my mother's health improve or deteriorate?'

The symbol in the square from line 25 and column 28 was oracle 20 — Pisces (the fishes). The corresponding column in Oracle 20 was her answer: 'It is useless to look for relief from medicine unless it is skilfully applied'.

This confirmed precisely what she was facing in seeking help for her mother. They had run into a series of physicians who were inadequate in relieving her pain and suffering through traditional examination and prescription of medicine. My friend was considering non-traditional help through homeopathic medicine; however, the answer presented the same dilemma — how to find a skilful physician, either traditional or non-traditional, within the limitations of the health service. The Enquirer's mother has experienced continued deterioration as of this writing since she has been unable to find anyone medically skilful.

1.
Venus/Moon

1	★ ★ ★ ★ ★	As the glorious sun eclipses the light of the stars, so will the partner of your bed be accounted the fairest among women.
2	★★ ★ ★ ★ ★	She shall have sons and daughters.
3	★ ★★ ★ ★ ★	Your friend is in good health; his thoughts are, at present, bent on you.
4	★ ★ ★★ ★ ★	You have no enemies who can in any degree injure you.
5	★ ★ ★ ★★ ★	Choose that for which your genius is best adapted.

6	★ ★ ★ ★ ★★	Set not your mind on searching after that which has been hidden but attend diligently to the duties of your calling.
7	★★ ★★ ★ ★ ★	Choose right trusty companions for your intended journey, and no ill can befall you.
8	★ ★★ ★★ ★ ★	Despair not; your love will meet its due reward.
9	★ ★ ★★ ★★ ★	Take not the advice of ignorant pretenders to the art of healing, but inquire immediately with qualified authorities.
10	★ ★ ★ ★★ ★★	Your husband will follow arms.
11	★ ★ ★★ ★ ★★	Praise the virtuous and heed not evil reports.
12	★ ★★ ★ ★★ ★	Be prepared for any change of fortune which may happen.
13	★★ ★ ★★ ★ ★	A speedy marriage is signified.

14	★ ★★ ★ ★ ★★	Although Fortune now turns her back upon you, your own efforts will soon enable you to triumph over her unpredictable temperament.
15	★★ ★ ★ ★★ ★	Bestow careful cultivation on the sapling, and when the tree arrives at maturity it will produce good fruit.
16	★★ ★ ★ ★ ★★	Let not busy and meddling persons who call themselves friends disturb the happiness of the married pair.
17	★★ ★★ ★★ ★ ★	Take heed that you give no just cause for your beloved to prove unfaithful to you.
18	★ ★★ ★★ ★★ ★	No impediment will be thrown in the way of the individual's quick return.
19	★ ★ ★★ ★★ ★★	The sceptre of power will be wrested from the conqueror.
20	★ ★★ ★ ★★ ★★	The recovery of your goods will be unexpected.
21	★ ★★ ★★ ★ ★★	When you have tested your friend, you may truly trust and value him.

22	★ ★ ★ ★ ★ ★ ★ ★	How do you expect to live in the remembrance of your fellow mortals, seeing your deeds are evil?
23	★ ★ ★ ★ ★ ★ ★ ★	Let not whimsy mar your happiness.
24	★ ★ ★ ★ ★ ★ ★ ★	Be not buoyed up by hopes of inheriting property which you have not earned.
25	★ ★ ★ ★ ★ ★ ★ ★	Be wise and success will follow.
26	★ ★ ★ ★ ★ ★ ★ ★	Be contented with your present fortune.
27	★ ★ ★ ★ ★ ★ ★ ★ ★	Fortune favours the brave and enterprising.
28	★ ★ ★ ★ ★ ★ ★ ★ ★	Your adversary will cheat you on the first opportunity.
29	★ ★ ★ ★ ★ ★ ★ ★ ★	Justice is blind, but not always deaf, for in many instances she loves to listen to the sweet ringing of gold and silver.

30	★★ ★★ ★★ ★ ★★	Avoid entering into the land of strangers.
31	★ ★★ ★★ ★★ ★★	As your youth may have been virtuous, so will old age prove respected and happy.
32	★★ ★★ ★★ ★★ ★★	The captive will speedily cease to breathe the foul air of a prison cell; let him use his freedom wisely.

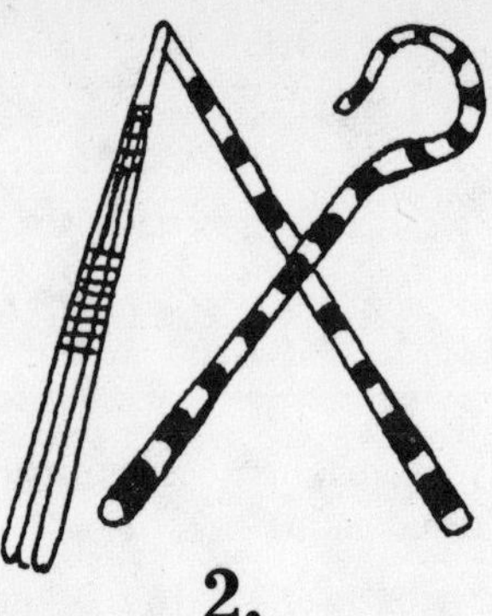

2.
Crossed keys

1	★ ★ ★ ★ ★	The door of the prison will soon be unlocked.
2	★★ ★ ★ ★ ★	Consider your present situation, whether it be right for you to marry.
3	★ ★★ ★ ★ ★	She shall have a son who will gain much wealth and honour.
4	★ ★ ★★ ★ ★	Your friends are well and are now occupied in promoting your welfare.
5	★ ★ ★ ★★ ★	You have, and ought to continue to be on your guard.

6	★ ★ ★ ★ ★★	Choose that of your richest relative.
7	★★ ★★ ★ ★ ★	Disappointment and irritation will plague you if you neglect your calling to seek after that which is beyond your power to find.
8	★ ★★ ★★ ★ ★	Implore the aid of Divine guidance before you set foot outside the threshold of your house.
9	★ ★ ★★ ★★ ★	The heart of your beloved yearns for you.
10	★ ★ ★ ★★ ★★	Let proper medicines be prescribed for the patient and certain recovery will follow.
11	★ ★ ★★ ★ ★★	Your husband will have many virtues, but also some faults; teach him to correct the latter and fortune will attend you both.
12	★ ★★ ★ ★★ ★	Your character will be proof against every unfavourable report.
13	★★ ★ ★★ ★ ★	Allow your heart to be lifted under your misfortunes, for prosperity will return to you in due season.

<table>
<tr><td>14</td><td>★
★★
★
★
★★</td><td>The signification is increase of riches.</td></tr>
<tr><td>15</td><td>★★
★
★
★★
★</td><td>Recovery from your misfortunes will be gradual, but neglect no opportunity of honestly advancing your own interests.</td></tr>
<tr><td>16</td><td>★★
★
★
★
★★</td><td>If you wish your children to be happy, let your theory and practice favour virtuous conduct.</td></tr>
<tr><td>17</td><td>★★
★★
★★
★
★</td><td>If misfortunes occur, bear them with fortitude and happiness will be the certain result.</td></tr>
<tr><td>18</td><td>★
★★
★★
★★
★</td><td>Be constant, and fear not.</td></tr>
<tr><td>19</td><td>★
★
★★
★★
★★</td><td>Matters which concern the absentee's future happiness prevent his immediate return.</td></tr>
<tr><td>20</td><td>★
★★
★
★★
★★</td><td>A conqueror of noble mind and mighty power shall spring from low condition; he will break the chains of the oppressed, and will give liberty to the nations.</td></tr>
<tr><td>21</td><td>★
★★
★★
★
★★</td><td>The thief will be detected in the midst of his career.</td></tr>
</table>

22	★★ ★ ★ ★★ ★★	If your friend has in one circumstance proved deceitful, trust him not a second time.
23	★★ ★ ★★ ★ ★★	The deeds of the offender will be held in damnation by posterity.
24	★★ ★★ ★ ★ ★★	Take heed that greed prove not the bane of your happiness.
25	★★ ★★ ★ ★★ ★	The will of a stranger may be written in your favour.
26	★★ ★ ★★ ★★ ★	Be not discouraged by adverse circumstances.
27	★★ ★★ ★★ ★★ ★	Be just in your dealings and trust to Divine guidance for advancement.
28	★★ ★ ★★ ★★ ★★	Nothing ventured, nothing gained!
29	★★ ★★ ★ ★★ ★★	Bet nothing on the result of a game played by others.

30	★★ ★★ ★★ ★ ★★	God will support you in a good cause.
31	★ ★★ ★★ ★★ ★★	Your wealth will not be gained in a strange land.
32	★★ ★★ ★★ ★★ ★★	The end of dissipation is speedy death; avoid this and live long.

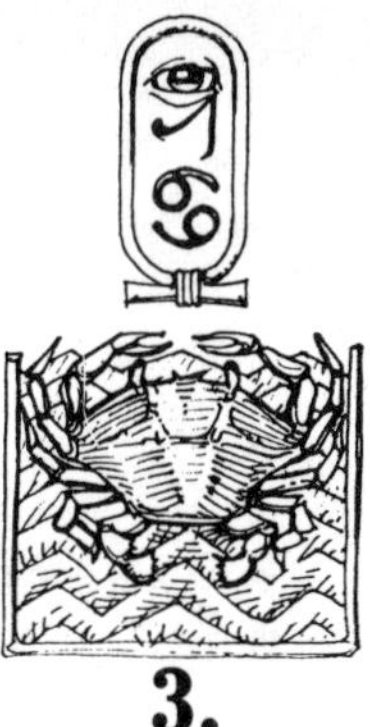

3. Cancer

1	★ ★ ★ ★ ★	Early to bed, early to rise, makes a man healthy, wealthy and wise.
2	★ ★ ★ ★ ★ ★	The prisoner will speedily be released.
3	★ ★ ★ ★ ★ ★	Good temper and fidelity are all you may depend on.
4	★ ★ ★ ★ ★ ★	She shall have a daughter who will inherit all her mother's virtues.
5	★ ★ ★ ★ ★ ★	Sickness is not entirely absent from the mansion of those whom you enquire after; they say that your presence would be agreeable.

6	★ ★ ★ ★ ★★	You have an enemy who will attempt to harm you.
7	★★ ★★ ★ ★ ★	Tread in your parent's footsteps.
8	★ ★★ ★★ ★ ★	Spend not your energy seeking after that which is not.
9	★ ★ ★★ ★★ ★	Before you go abroad put your affairs in order, and when you return from your journey, you shall find your goods secure.
10	★ ★ ★ ★★ ★★	The love which you bear each other will be rewarded by a happy marriage.
11	★ ★ ★★ ★ ★★	As you hope for a speedy recovery, follow not the advice of the meddlesome charlatan.
12	★ ★★ ★ ★★ ★	The man of your heart will not be rich, but will be well-favoured and he will give you every satisfaction.
13	★★ ★ ★★ ★ ★	No man ever was, or ever will be without enemies, but those who slander you shall be taken in their own nets.

14	★ ★★ ★ ★ ★★	If you go to a far country your Fate will be to undergo many perils.
15	★★ ★ ★ ★★ ★	It portends death among your enemies.
16	★★ ★ ★ ★ ★★	There are many who sink under the burdens of this life; be not one of them, but exert yourself and prosper.
17	★★ ★★ ★★ ★ ★	As you desire prosperity and happiness for your children, teach them to avoid evil company.
18	★ ★★ ★★ ★★ ★	By this marriage, if you are wise, you will gain much happiness.
19	★ ★ ★★ ★★ ★★	Give no credit to the insinuation that your beloved will prove untrue.
20	★ ★★ ★ ★★ ★★	The traveller will soon return in good health.
21	★ ★★ ★★ ★ ★★	The Islanders who have long swayed the sceptre of the ocean shall cease to conquer, but they will become the instructors of mankind.

22	★ ★ ★ ★ ★ ★ ★ ★	Let not your hopes of recovering what you have lost be too optimistic.
23	★ ★ ★ ★ ★ ★ ★ ★	If you see the man whom you call your friend carry himself deceitfully or dishonestly towards others, deceive not yourself by thinking he will be faithful to you.
24	★ ★ ★ ★ ★ ★ ★ ★	Let not the love of fame blind you to the interests of your fellow creatures.
25	★ ★ ★ ★ ★ ★ ★ ★	You shall be happier than up to now.
26	★ ★ ★ ★ ★ ★ ★ ★	Be contented with what you already have.
27	★ ★ ★ ★ ★ ★ ★ ★ ★	Fortune will shower her favours on you if you combine justice with prudence.
28	★ ★ ★ ★ ★ ★ ★ ★ ★	Still hope! Never despair.
29	★ ★ ★ ★ ★ ★ ★ ★ ★	Lose not your time and money by expecting from the lottery what you may easily obtain from your business.

30	★★ ★★ ★★ ★ ★★	When your ready money is gone, go also; never borrow.
31	★ ★★ ★★ ★★ ★★	You shall have no gain in a lawsuit; therefore be wise and careful.
32	★★ ★★ ★★ ★★ ★★	In a strange land a happy marriage awaits you.

4.
Bird

1	★ ★ ★ ★ ★	You shall have to travel by sea, air, and land.
2	★★ ★ ★ ★ ★	Yes!
3	★ ★★ ★ ★ ★	He will at last be freed from the power of his enemies.
4	★ ★ ★★ ★ ★	You shall have a fortune with your partner.
5	★ ★ ★ ★★ ★	You shall be blessed with a son who, if duly instructed, will make your latter years honourable.

6	★ ★ ★ ★ ★ ★	Your friend enjoys perfect health and is presently writing to a relative.
7	★ ★ ★ ★ ★ ★ ★	A secret enemy will endeavour to undermine your happiness.
8	★ ★ ★ ★ ★ ★ ★	Choose one which with a little labour will afford you a comfortable subsistence.
9	★ ★ ★ ★ ★ ★ ★	Your business will provide you a mine of wealth if you are careful and utilize your time wisely.
10	★ ★ ★ ★ ★ ★ ★	Your journey will be safe and its goal will be attained.
11	★ ★ ★ ★ ★ ★ ★	Your love is not disregarded.
12	★ ★ ★ ★ ★ ★ ★	The patient will recover; but let this illness be a warning to keep due guard over his health in the future.
13	★ ★ ★ ★ ★ ★ ★	You shall wed a man on whom great honours will be conferred.

14	★ ★★ ★ ★ ★★	See that you deserve to be well spoken of.
15	★★ ★ ★ ★★ ★	Great fluctuation await the traveller.
16	★★ ★ ★ ★ ★★	The signification is disaster among your foes.
17	★★ ★★ ★★ ★ ★	Consider whether you are not the cause of your misfortunes; if so, be more prudent in the future.
18	★ ★★ ★★ ★★ ★	Misery will be the sure Fate of your children if their morals be corrupted by evil communication.
19	★ ★ ★★ ★★ ★★	Delay not this union as your happiness would be jeopardized.
20	★ ★★ ★ ★★ ★★	You shall reign paramount in the affections of the one whom you love.
21	★ ★★ ★★ ★ ★★	Let not impatience urge too speedy a return.

22	★★ ★ ★ ★★ ★★	As knowledge is diffused throughout the world, men of all conditions, of every colour, and in every clime, will become free.
23	★★ ★ ★★ ★ ★★	With trouble and expense you may gain your lost goods.
24	★★ ★★ ★ ★ ★★	Honesty is the only bond of true friendship.
25	★★ ★★ ★ ★★ ★	Seek not fame in the cannon's mouth.
26	★★ ★ ★★ ★★ ★	Supreme happiness is seldom the Fate of mortal man.
27	★★ ★★ ★★ ★★ ★	You are the favourite of fortune.
28	★★ ★ ★★ ★★ ★★	Weigh well the probable result of your present intentions.
29	★★ ★★ ★ ★★ ★★	By righteous conduct, you are sure to rise.

30	★★ ★★ ★★ ★ ★★	Save pennies; the pounds will save themselves.
31	★ ★★ ★★ ★★ ★★	Never lend at the gaming table.
32	★★ ★★ ★★ ★★ ★★	Rather sacrifice a pound than throw away a fiver in litigation.

5.
Compass & Square

1	★ ★ ★ ★ ★	Act wisely, justly, and trouble not the judges of the land.
2	★ ★ ★ ★ ★ ★	It would be rash to embark for a foreign land.
3	★ ★ ★ ★ ★ ★	Some men are old even at thirty; take care of your health and you will see seventy or more.
4	★ ★ ★ ★ ★ ★	The captive's heart will be made glad.
5	★ ★ ★ ★ ★ ★	If you are careful, you will marry exceedingly well.

6	★ ★ ★ ★ ★★	Your wife shall have two daughters whose virtues and beauty will be the theme of general praise.
7	★★ ★★ ★ ★ ★	Your friends are now toasting and wishing you health and happiness.
8	★ ★★ ★★ ★ ★	Beware false friends!
9	★ ★ ★★ ★★ ★	You ought to budget and save.
10	★ ★ ★ ★★ ★★	Vain thing! Flatter not yourself with the hopes of finding silver and gold in hidden places.
11	★ ★ ★★ ★ ★★	Let the companion of your journey be honest as well as brave.
12	★ ★★ ★ ★★ ★	Heed not, if disappointment should mar your present hopes.
13	★★ ★ ★★ ★ ★	The patient's health will be restored.

14	★ ★★ ★ ★ ★★	You shall wed a man in an exalted station.
15	★★ ★ ★ ★★ ★	Act justly and defy misfortune.
16	★★ ★ ★ ★ ★★	If you set forth from the land of your fathers, expect great changes.
17	★★ ★★ ★★ ★ ★	Your dream says be diligent in your business.
18	★ ★★ ★★ ★★ ★	Mankind is often the judge of its own fortunes; be honest, and fail not to take advantage of every circumstance which may improve yours.
19	★ ★ ★★ ★★ ★★	Destroy the seeds of vice, and implant those of virtue in the minds of your children, and happiness will be the certain result.
20	★ ★★ ★ ★★ ★★	Consider whether you ought to marry now.
21	★ ★★ ★★ ★ ★★	Endurance on your part will bring its due return.

<table>
<tr><td>22</td><td>★★
★
★
★★
★★</td><td>When the object is accomplished, the traveller will assuredly return.</td></tr>
<tr><td>23</td><td>★★
★
★★
★
★★</td><td>A colony of outcasts will break their chains, and obtain great dominion.</td></tr>
<tr><td>24</td><td>★★
★★
★
★
★★</td><td>Let not the loss of this thing press heavily on your mind.</td></tr>
<tr><td>25</td><td>★★
★★
★
★★
★</td><td>Rely not on those self-styled friends who, like summer flies, buzz about you in your prosperity.</td></tr>
<tr><td>26</td><td>★★
★
★★
★★
★</td><td>A cottage and contentment give more enjoyment than the princely palace of the conqueror of kingdoms.</td></tr>
<tr><td>27</td><td>★★
★★
★★
★★
★</td><td>Be contented with your lot, and there is little doubt of your happiness.</td></tr>
<tr><td>28</td><td>★★
★
★★
★★
★★</td><td>Be content; let tomorrow provide for itself.</td></tr>
<tr><td>29</td><td>★★
★★
★
★★
★★</td><td>As you hope for success, act not unjustly towards others.</td></tr>
</table>

30	★★ ★★ ★★ ★ ★★	Do not discard present aspects toward pursuing a vision.
31	★ ★★ ★★ ★★ ★★	In your family be liberal, but in your business be conservative.
32	★★ ★★ ★★ ★★ ★★	Maintain your balance at the gaming table.

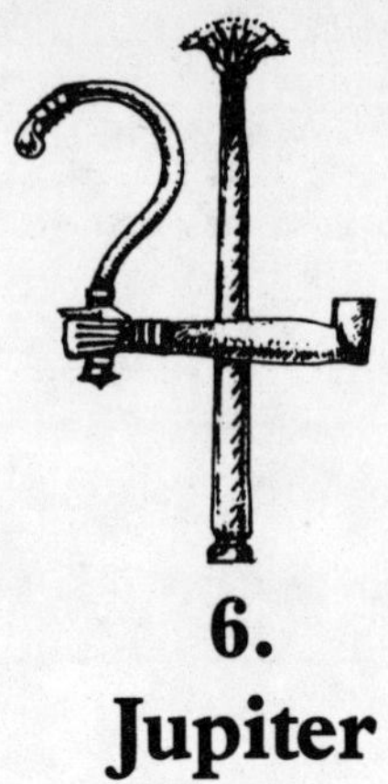

6.
Jupiter

1	★ ★ ★ ★ ★	Money may be staked but never risk goods and lands at the gaming tables.
2	★★ ★ ★ ★ ★	You shall be involved in a suit but will speedily extricate yourself.
3	★ ★★ ★ ★ ★	You will be prosperous in your journey but do not stay abroad longer than is necessary.
4	★ ★ ★★ ★ ★	Rise early, work or walk before you eat, and doubt it not.
5	★ ★ ★ ★★ ★	The prisoner will soon have cause to rejoice.

<table>
<tr><td>6</td><td>★
★
★
★
★★</td><td>Your partner will be rich, but she will also be proud.</td></tr>
<tr><td>7</td><td>★★
★★
★
★
★</td><td>She shall bear a son whose talents will be of the first order; see that they be well directed.</td></tr>
<tr><td>8</td><td>★
★★
★★
★
★</td><td>The health of those you love is good; they enjoy the sweets of rural happiness, and wish that you were with them.</td></tr>
<tr><td>9</td><td>★
★
★★
★★
★</td><td>You have enemies, but they will have no power over you.</td></tr>
<tr><td>10</td><td>★
★
★
★★
★★</td><td>Meddle not with the laws of the land.</td></tr>
<tr><td>11</td><td>★
★
★★
★
★★</td><td>If you pay attention to all the facets of your calling, a fortune awaits you greater than any treasure within the country in which you reside.</td></tr>
<tr><td>12</td><td>★
★★
★
★★
★</td><td>Tempt not those whom you meet or deal with by showing them your money bags.</td></tr>
<tr><td>13</td><td>★★
★
★★
★
★</td><td>If your love is true, it will be duly appreciated.</td></tr>
</table>

14	★ ★★ ★ ★ ★★	A speedy recovery will be the consequence of properly applied remedies.
15	★★ ★ ★ ★★ ★	Your husband will be in all respects a good man; it will be his intention to render you the happiest of your sex.
16	★★ ★ ★ ★ ★★	Let your conduct be unimpeachable and you may defy the slanderous charges.
17	★★ ★★ ★★ ★ ★	Be prudent and do not depend entirely on your present good fortune.
18	★ ★★ ★★ ★★ ★	You were called upon in your vision to be charitable and to give some of your abundance, in charity, to the poor.
19	★ ★ ★★ ★★ ★★	Your present misfortunes shall have but little influence on your future good fortune.
20	★ ★★ ★ ★★ ★★	When you are cold in your grave, your name will be greatly honoured by your children.
21	★ ★★ ★★ ★ ★★	By wedding this person you ensure happiness for a long time.

22	★★ ★ ★ ★★ ★★	If your beloved has proved inconstant to another, think not that she will prove faithful to you.
23	★★ ★ ★★ ★ ★★	Love prompts the traveller's speedy return to his home.
24	★★ ★★ ★ ★ ★★	An infant nation shall, by the wisdom of its councils, become the centre of commerce and the arts.
25	★★ ★★ ★ ★★ ★	Your goods may soon be recovered.
26	★★ ★ ★★ ★★ ★	Declare that you are poor and see how many friends will run to aid you.
27	★★ ★★ ★★ ★★ ★	Be not the trumpeter of your own fame; if your deeds are truly great, posterity will not overlook them.
28	★★ ★ ★★ ★★ ★★	Whatever occurs, do not become discontented.
29	★★ ★★ ★ ★★ ★★	Hope for the best, but make up your mind to bear with the worst that might happen.

30	★★ ★★ ★★ ★ ★★	Save yourself the trouble and expense of entering into rash and unprofitable speculation.
31	★ ★★ ★★ ★★ ★★	Be content and ignore the urge toward ambition.
32	★★ ★★ ★★ ★★ ★★	Economy and thriftiness can lead to stinginess but also the means to an end.

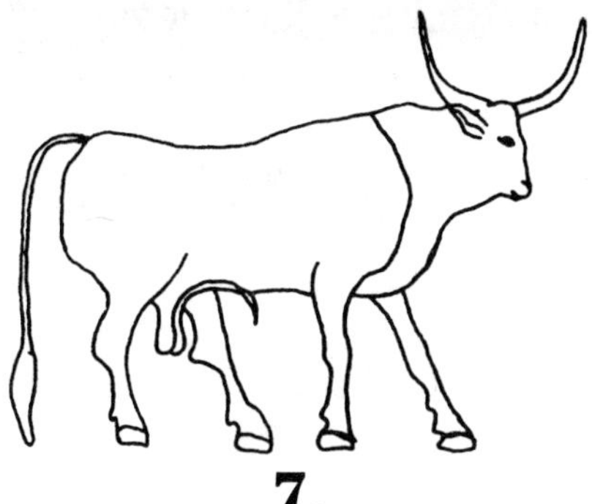

7.
Taurus

1	★ ★ ★ ★ ★	Be like the bee and you shall reap the honey of your labours.
2	★ ★ ★ ★ ★ ★	You will mar it wondrously.
3	★ ★ ★ ★ ★ ★	Avoiding this evil depends greatly on yourself.
4	★ ★ ★ ★ ★ ★	The journey will be to your advantage.
5	★ ★ ★ ★ ★ ★	Long life depends greatly on moderation.

6	★ ★ ★ ★ ★★	He who inhabits the cell will escape.
7	★★ ★★ ★ ★ ★	Your first partner will be poor, handsome, and chaste; the second, exactly the reverse.
8	★ ★★ ★★ ★ ★	A daughter will be born to you who will possess much beauty which may prove an impediment to her if early vanity is not duly checked.
9	★ ★ ★★ ★★ ★	Your friends are not in ill health but all things are not presently agreeable to them.
10	★ ★ ★ ★★ ★★	Envious people will endeavour to impede your passage through life.
11	★ ★ ★★ ★ ★★	Avoid tools with a sharp cutting edge!
12	★ ★★ ★ ★★ ★	Be diligent in your calling and do not deceive yourself with false hopes.
13	★★ ★ ★★ ★ ★	As you journey along, commend yourself to God and He will watch over you.

14	★ ★★ ★ ★ ★★	If you are discreet you shall gain the object on which your heart is fixed.
15	★★ ★ ★ ★★ ★	Let the advice of the experienced be taken and health will speedily be restored.
16	★★ ★ ★ ★ ★★	Your shall marry a man whose mind will be elevated above his condition. It will be your duty sometimes to restrain him.
17	★★ ★★ ★★ ★ ★	It will; but out of their own mouths will your slanderers be condemned.
18	★ ★★ ★★ ★★ ★	Despair not; though fortune should desert you, it will be but for a time.
19	★ ★ ★★ ★★ ★★	You were told in your vision that your present undertaking will prosper if you are cautious and vigilant.
20	★ ★★ ★ ★★ ★★	Cheer your heart; prosperity will soon visit you.
21	★ ★★ ★★ ★ ★★	Choose those callings for your children for which their talents are adapted; teach them to be virtuous and careful, and leave the rest to God.

22	★★ ★ ★ ★★ ★★	Enter not into situations in which you have not well considered the end.
23	★★ ★ ★★ ★ ★★	Your beloved merits all your confidence.
24	★★ ★★ ★ ★ ★★	Nothing can happen to retard the individual's speedy arrival.
25	★★ ★★ ★ ★★ ★	The rank weeds which have long infested the gardens of the south will be plucked out, and the tree of liberty will flourish luxuriantly in their stead.
26	★★ ★ ★★ ★★ ★	Leave no means untried to detect the thief.
27	★★ ★★ ★★ ★★ ★	The man who most declares his readiness to befriend you will be the first to desert you at the first adversity.
28	★★ ★ ★★ ★★ ★★	Dip not your laurels in the blood of the vanquished.
29	★★ ★★ ★ ★★ ★★	Let not the irritation of your temper mar your happiness.

30	★★ ★★ ★★ ★ ★★	Be courteous to your kinsman and he will remember you.
31	★ ★★ ★★ ★★ ★★	Take the advice of your best friend before proceeding.
32	★★ ★★ ★★ ★★ ★★	You shall long be prosperous and ought therefore be content; in the end your unbounded ambition will be your ruin.

8.
Ladder

1	★ ★ ★ ★ ★	You shall be fortunate and meet with advancement in your business.
2	★★ ★ ★ ★ ★	Yes.
3	★ ★★ ★ ★ ★	Do you expect to plunge your hand into the fire and not be burnt?
4	★ ★ ★★ ★ ★	Do as you would be done by and you will save much time and money.
5	★ ★ ★ ★★ ★	Venture not far from home!

<table>
<tr><td>6</td><td>★
★
★
★
★ ★</td><td>Go to bed with the lamb, rise with the lark, and doubt it not.</td></tr>
<tr><td>7</td><td>★ ★
★ ★
★
★
★</td><td>A friend will procure his speedy release.</td></tr>
<tr><td>8</td><td>★
★ ★
★ ★
★
★</td><td>Your partner's temper will be exemplary; take care in all cases that you imitate it.</td></tr>
<tr><td>9</td><td>★
★
★ ★
★ ★
★</td><td>Your wife shall have a son who will be both learned and wise.</td></tr>
<tr><td>10</td><td>★
★
★
★ ★
★ ★</td><td>Amusement, at present, occupies the attention of your friends.</td></tr>
<tr><td>11</td><td>★
★
★ ★
★
★ ★</td><td>You have an enemy but you and your fortune are safe from every attempt at doing you harm.</td></tr>
<tr><td>12</td><td>★
★ ★
★
★ ★
★</td><td>If you are wise you will not decline rural happiness.</td></tr>
<tr><td>13</td><td>★ ★
★
★ ★
★
★</td><td>A treasure awaits you of which you have little expectation.</td></tr>
</table>

14	★ ★★ ★ ★ ★★	Danger may threaten you if you remain long in a strange land.
15	★★ ★ ★ ★★ ★	The hand of your beloved will ultimately reward your affection.
16	★★ ★ ★ ★ ★★	Though the patient escape this time, let him not presume on the strength of his constitution.
17	★★ ★★ ★★ ★ ★	By your marriage you will be envied by others of your sex.
18	★ ★★ ★★ ★★ ★	Be prudent and courteous to all men and the arrows of slander will be blunted before they reach thee.
19	★ ★ ★★ ★★ ★★	It will be your Fate to see many changes.
20	★ ★★ ★ ★★ ★★	You dream of a wedding which will soon take place.
21	★ ★★ ★★ ★ ★★	See that your misfortunes urge you not on to drunkenness; if so, you may never recover from them.

22	★★ ★ ★ ★★ ★★	In the training of your offspring, let discipline be strict, but not severe; lose no opportunity of improving their understandings, and in the plentitude of their happiness they will bless thee.
23	★★ ★ ★★ ★ ★★	It behoves the party to make a light matter of any impediments which may be thrown in the way of his happiness.
24	★★ ★★ ★ ★ ★★	There is no just cause why you should question the fidelity of your beloved.
25	★★ ★★ ★ ★★ ★	Though the individual's stay abroad is long, it will be greatly to his advantage.
26	★★ ★ ★★ ★★ ★	A powerful people will regain the power they have lost when their minds are united toward intelligent action rather than dissipation.
27	★★ ★★ ★★ ★★ ★	Take not away the life of the man who has injured you.
28	★★ ★ ★★ ★★ ★★	Avoid laying too great a tax on the patience of your friends; this is the way to preserve them.
29	★★ ★★ ★ ★★ ★★	Be not eager to raise the monument of your own fame.

30	★★ ★★ ★★ ★ ★★	Matrimony will afford you much happiness.
31	★ ★★ ★★ ★★ ★★	Be civil to every man; you know not who may prove your friend.
32	★★ ★★ ★★ ★★ ★★	Be not purse-proud, nor vainglorious in the midst of your good fortune.

9.
Star

1	★ ★ ★ ★ ★	Let the star of prudence guide you in your course.
2	★ ★ ★ ★ ★ ★	There is a tide in the affairs of men which, taken advantage of, leads on to fortune.
3	★ ★ ★ ★ ★ ★	You shall be content and happy.
4	★ ★ ★ ★ ★ ★	Taste not! Touch not! Handle not!
5	★ ★ ★ ★ ★ ★	If you dislike the law, meddle not with it.

6	★ ★ ★ ★ ★★	When you have an opportunity you may proceed confidently.
7	★★ ★★ ★ ★ ★	Old age is attained only by men who have the resolution to live temperately.
8	★ ★★ ★★ ★ ★	The prisoner will soon be welcomed home although he now smarts under the power of his enemies.
9	★ ★ ★★ ★★ ★	You shall have a handsome partner.
10	★ ★ ★ ★★ ★★	She shall have a son whose dutiful conduct in his youth will ensure you comfort in your old age.
11	★ ★ ★★ ★ ★★	Your friends are now occupied in devotional duties.
12	★ ★★ ★ ★★ ★	Enemies will endeavour to subvert your reputation.
13	★★ ★ ★★ ★ ★	Sell strong liquor; but be careful of often trying their strength upon yourself.

14	★ ★ ★ ★ ★ ★ ★	A rich treasure awaits you.
15	★ ★ ★ ★ ★ ★ ★	No accident will befall you.
16	★ ★ ★ ★ ★ ★ ★	You are more beloved than you can be now aware of.
17	★ ★ ★ ★ ★ ★ ★ ★	The afflicted will soon be freed from pain.
18	★ ★ ★ ★ ★ ★ ★ ★	Your husband will inherit great riches.
19	★ ★ ★ ★ ★ ★ ★ ★	You will be maligned, but when your slanderers are confronted, they will be put to shame.
20	★ ★ ★ ★ ★ ★ ★ ★	Political changes will change your fortune.
21	★ ★ ★ ★ ★ ★ ★ ★	Your vision says that gifts will be made unto you.

22	★★ ★ ★ ★★ ★★	Strong drink may cheer your heart now and make you forget your sorrows for a short time but in the end they will incapacitate you for the enjoyment of prosperity.
23	★★ ★ ★★ ★ ★★	Lose no opportunity of pointing out to your children the deeds of virtuous men and in the emulation of them they will do honour to principles.
24	★★ ★★ ★ ★ ★★	Much prosperity will come to the wedded pair.
25	★★ ★★ ★ ★★ ★	Harbour not unjust suspicions.
26	★★ ★ ★★ ★★ ★	When the individual has settled his affairs he will lose no time in returning to his own country.
27	★★ ★★ ★★ ★★ ★	The deceiver of his people will be caught in the meshes of the cunningly contrived net which he himself has woven.
28	★★ ★ ★★ ★★ ★★	Give not the thief the chance of robbing you again.
29	★★ ★★ ★ ★★ ★★	Consider well before you tell your secret, whether your friend can keep it.

30	★★ ★★ ★★ ★ ★★	Do good, and if mankind should fail to remember you, you are still their benefactor.
31	★ ★★ ★★ ★★ ★★	Think not of enjoying happiness until your conduct has been reformed.
32	★★ ★★ ★★ ★★ ★★	Be a friend to yourself — depend not on others.

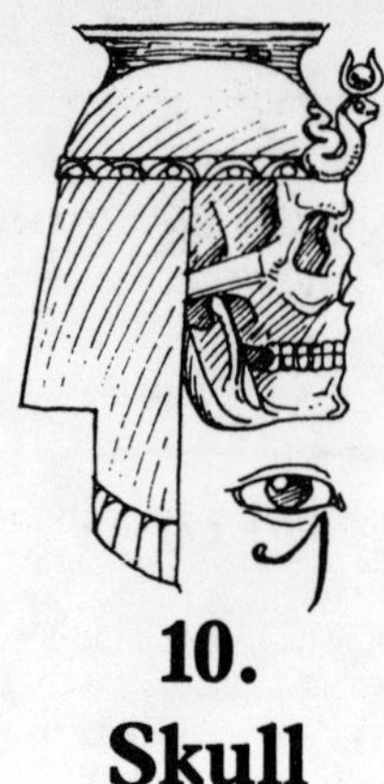

10.
Skull

1	★ ★ ★ ★ ★	Wish not for the death of your kinsman that you may inherit his worldly goods.
2	★★ ★ ★ ★ ★	Greed is the ruin of thousands.
3	★ ★★ ★ ★ ★	Perseverance conquers every impediment.
4	★ ★ ★★ ★ ★	You are too ambitious.
5	★ ★ ★ ★★ ★	You may be successful — millions have been ruined.

6	★ ★ ★ ★ ★ ★	Your Fate is to litigate, but in the end you will be successful.
7	★ ★ ★ ★ ★ ★ ★	If you remain from your home for long, your fortune will not prosper.
8	★ ★ ★ ★ ★ ★ ★	Drunkenness brings on premature old age; avoid it, and you will live long.
9	★ ★ ★ ★ ★ ★ ★	With much difficulty he will obtain a discharge from his bondage.
10	★ ★ ★ ★ ★ ★ ★	Your partner will, in time, have much money; use it well.
11	★ ★ ★ ★ ★ ★ ★	A daughter will be born unto you who will be highly honoured and respected.
12	★ ★ ★ ★ ★ ★ ★	Your friend is well; he now drinks to your health.
13	★ ★ ★ ★ ★ ★ ★	You have enemies, but you shall defeat them and they will be overwhelmed with shame.

14	★ ★★ ★ ★ ★★	You may make a fortune by dealing in precious stones.
15	★★ ★ ★ ★★ ★	Health will be the richest treasure you can ever possess.
16	★★ ★ ★ ★ ★★	Safety and success in your travels will greatly depend upon your conduct towards those whom you meet.
17	★★ ★★ ★★ ★ ★	Persevere and do not give up your position lightly.
18	★ ★★ ★★ ★★ ★	Let all proper means be used and a speedy end will be put to the patient's disorder.
19	★ ★ ★★ ★★ ★★	By marriage your fortune and happiness will be greatly increased.
20	★ ★★ ★ ★★ ★★	When the evil report reaches your ears, instantly seek the slanderer out and he will be confounded in your presence.
21	★ ★★ ★★ ★ ★★	Whatever changes you may undergo, they will be for your benefit.

22	★★ ★ ★ ★★ ★★	It says that favours will be conferred on you forthwith.
23	★★ ★ ★★ ★ ★★	As you hope for lasting prosperity, drown not your cares in strong drink; if you do, your prospects will be forever blasted.
24	★★ ★★ ★ ★ ★★	Their happiness will depend solely on the instruction which you give them.
25	★★ ★★ ★ ★★ ★	Be discreet in the associations which you form for life.
26	★★ ★ ★★ ★★ ★	The suspicious lover is the destroyer of his own peace.
27	★★ ★★ ★★ ★★ ★	When the absentee returns, it will be with joy and honour.
28	★★ ★ ★★ ★★ ★★	Ignorance and oppression, like a thick mist on the mountain top, will be gradually dispersed, as the sun of knowledge enlightens the understanding of men.
29	★★ ★★ ★ ★★ ★★	Admonish, but pursue not unto death, him who has injured you.

No.	Stars	Answer
30	★★ ★★ ★★ ★ ★★	Never trust those men who swear friendship to you over the cup of drunkenness.
31	★ ★★ ★★ ★★ ★★	The good deeds of men are frequently traced on sand; their bad ones engraved on marble.
32	★★ ★★ ★★ ★★ ★★	Set not your heart on pleasure derived from earthly objects.

11.
Cornucopia

1	★ ★ ★ ★ ★	Peace and plenty will be your certain allotment if you are industrious.
2	★★ ★ ★ ★ ★	Will you wait for dead men's old shoes? Your own exertions might procure you new ones.
3	★ ★★ ★ ★ ★	Let prudence guide you in this affair.
4	★ ★ ★★ ★ ★	Promotion depends entirely on yourself.
5	★ ★ ★ ★★ ★	Doubt it not!

6	★ ★ ★ ★ ★ ★	The chances are three to one against you.
7	★ ★ ★ ★ ★ ★ ★	Avoid the law as you would the plague.
8	★ ★ ★ ★ ★ ★ ★	In another country fortune will shower her favours on you.
9	★ ★ ★ ★ ★ ★ ★	Length of your days depends greatly on your habits; if you are not intemperate in gluttony and drink you will live long.
10	★ ★ ★ ★ ★ ★ ★	The prisoner will find much difficulty in obtaining pardon.
11	★ ★ ★ ★ ★ ★ ★	You will marry into a rich and respectable family.
12	★ ★ ★ ★ ★ ★ ★	A beautiful male child will be born unto you.
13	★ ★ ★ ★ ★ ★ ★	Your friend is happier and in better health than usual and is preparing for a journey.

<table>
<tr><td>14</td><td>★
★ ★
★
★
★ ★</td><td>You will be surrounded by secret enemies but they will be caught in the trap which they prepared for you.</td></tr>
<tr><td>15</td><td>★ ★
★
★
★ ★
★</td><td>Be a miller, but grind not the dignity of the poor.</td></tr>
<tr><td>16</td><td>★ ★
★
★
★
★ ★</td><td>You shall possess a rich mine out of which treasures shall be dug from time to time.</td></tr>
<tr><td>17</td><td>★ ★
★ ★
★ ★
★
★</td><td>Prosperity will surely serve you.</td></tr>
<tr><td>18</td><td>★
★ ★
★ ★
★ ★
★</td><td>Consider whether the object of your affections deserves your love.</td></tr>
<tr><td>19</td><td>★
★
★ ★
★ ★
★ ★</td><td>Fear not — the patient will recover.</td></tr>
<tr><td>20</td><td>★
★ ★
★
★ ★
★ ★</td><td>Your husband will be a man of honour and integrity.</td></tr>
<tr><td>21</td><td>★
★ ★
★ ★
★
★ ★</td><td>Your reputation will not be seriously injured by false charges.</td></tr>
</table>

22	★★ ★ ★ ★★ ★★	Look not on the present as the most important period of your life.
23	★★ ★ ★★ ★ ★★	It signifies prosperity to you and yours.
24	★★ ★★ ★ ★ ★★	When your misfortunes press hardest on you, be not dismayed, but endeavour to remove them.
25	★★ ★★ ★ ★★ ★	If your child is permitted to stray from the paths of virtue, you may expect that vice and misery will be his portion through life.
26	★★ ★ ★★ ★★ ★	Marriages entered into hastily end in sorrow — not so those which are wisely contracted.
27	★★ ★★ ★★ ★★ ★	The object of your affections will never requite your love with ingratitude.
28	★★ ★ ★★ ★★ ★★	Fear not but that the individual will speedily return.
29	★★ ★★ ★ ★★ ★★	Shouts of 'Freedom!' will resound throughout the halls which once were filled with the sighs and groans of despair.

30	★★ ★★ ★★ ★ ★★	Leave no means untried to make good your loss.
31	★ ★★ ★★ ★★ ★★	Beware lest the honeyed words of the hypocrite and the deceiver betray you into danger.
32	★★ ★★ ★★ ★★ ★★	Take good heed! Infamy is the certain share of the wicked man.

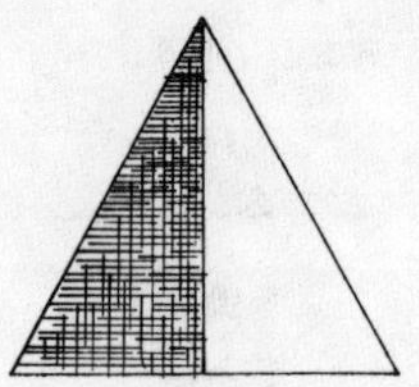

12. Pyramid

1	★ ★ ★ ★ ★	Your name will be handed down with the memory of your deeds to the most distant future.
2	★★ ★ ★ ★ ★	There is every prospect of happiness for you.
3	★ ★★ ★ ★ ★	Depend not entirely on the present intentions of your kinsman; they may alter.
4	★ ★ ★★ ★ ★	Success will depend much on perseverance.
5	★ ★ ★ ★★ ★	You shall meet with many obstacles, but at length you shall attain the highest earthly power and honour.

6	★ ★ ★ ★ ★★	Industry, perseverance and circumspection will accomplish your most optimistic wishes.
7	★★ ★★ ★ ★ ★	Play no games of risk.
8	★ ★★ ★★ ★ ★	Law is a two-edged sword which will assuredly smite you if you come within its reach.
9	★ ★ ★★ ★★ ★	Remain at home and you will do well.
10	★ ★ ★ ★★ ★★	A frugal diet will preserve your health and give you many days to live, while the midnight banquet may kill you straight.
11	★ ★ ★★ ★ ★★	Once more will the captive breathe the air of freedom.
12	★ ★★ ★ ★★ ★	Your partner will be strictly virtuous; see to it that you be likewise.
13	★★ ★ ★★ ★ ★	You shall have a son whose health during his childhood will require much care.

<table>
<tr><td>14</td><td>★
★★
★
★
★★</td><td>Your friends are making merry and wish you to form one of their circle.</td></tr>
<tr><td>15</td><td>★★
★
★
★★
★</td><td>You have; but they will be defeated.</td></tr>
<tr><td>16</td><td>★★
★
★
★
★★</td><td>You are cut out for an acrobat.</td></tr>
<tr><td>17</td><td>★★
★★
★★
★
★</td><td>Contentment is a richer treasure than any other you can find.</td></tr>
<tr><td>18</td><td>★
★★
★★
★★
★</td><td>Associate not with wicked companions and your journey will be accomplished in safety.</td></tr>
<tr><td>19</td><td>★
★
★★
★★
★★</td><td>Wait patiently, and your love will be requited in time.</td></tr>
<tr><td>20</td><td>★
★★
★
★★
★★</td><td>Let not old women, who pretend to medical knowledge, tamper with the patient's constitution.</td></tr>
<tr><td>21</td><td>★
★★
★★
★
★★</td><td>Your husband's conduct will be such as to merit from you every kindness.</td></tr>
</table>

22	★★ ★ ★ ★★ ★★	If you act prudently and uprightly, you need not fear the tongue of the slanderer.
23	★★ ★ ★★ ★ ★★	As the seasons vary, so will your fortune.
24	★★ ★★ ★ ★ ★★	It says, 'Let not the next opportunity escape of advancing your fortune'.
25	★★ ★★ ★ ★★ ★	Let not despair be added to the burden of your misfortunes, but hope that they will be removed in due time.
26	★★ ★ ★★ ★★ ★	If you gain the confidence of your children, you may lay the foundation of their happiness by teaching them to discriminate between good and evil.
27	★★ ★★ ★★ ★★ ★	If greed or mere lust prompt your marriage, expect not lasting happiness.
28	★★ ★ ★★ ★★ ★★	As the sun steadily pursues his glorious course in the heavens, so will your beloved remain constant to her vows.
29	★★ ★★ ★ ★★ ★★	You shall soon behold the face of the stranger.

30	★★ ★★ ★★ ★ ★★	A vast empire in the west will burst the chains which fetter it.
31	★ ★★ ★★ ★★ ★★	If you are careful the property may soon be found.
32	★★ ★★ ★★ ★★ ★★	The grip of the hand, the kiss on the cheek, and the vow of friendship over the flowing bowl are but as words traced on the sand of the seashore — trust them not.

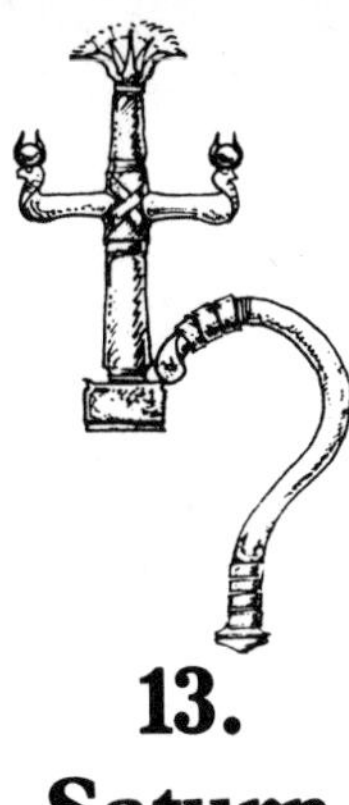

13. Saturn

1	★ ★ ★ ★ ★	Place not your confidence even in a friend as to put a weapon in his hand which he may turn upon you in the future.
2	★ ★ ★ ★ ★ ★	Your fame will resound to the farthest corners of the earth.
3	★ ★ ★ ★ ★ ★	Prosperity awaits you.
4	★ ★ ★ ★ ★ ★	Your own industry will supply every want; but if property be bequeathed to you, be thankful.
5	★ ★ ★ ★ ★ ★	If you manage discreetly, you shall be successful.

6	★ ★ ★ ★ ★★	You shall be preferred.
7	★★ ★★ ★ ★ ★	In ten years from this time (unless by too little dependence on yourself, you drive fortune from your door), you shall be called rich.
8	★ ★★ ★★ ★ ★	If you are wise, give to the poor what you are content to throw away on the turn of a card.
9	★ ★ ★★ ★★ ★	Law leaves little for the litigant; you will gain your cause, but the cost will be greater than it is worth.
10	★ ★ ★ ★★ ★★	Stay with your friends and you will escape many calamities.
11	★ ★ ★★ ★ ★★	The shipwrecked mariner may escape the raging gales and the thief the gallows, but sudden death is the sure Fate of the glutton and drunkard.
12	★ ★★ ★ ★★ ★	If much exertion be used he will obtain his liberty.
13	★★ ★ ★★ ★ ★	A rich and young person will be your partner.

14	★ ★★ ★ ★ ★★	She shall bear a son who will reflect much honour on his family.
15	★★ ★ ★ ★★ ★	Your friend is free from all bodily illness and now listens to the sweet sounds of music.
16	★★ ★ ★ ★ ★★	The enemies who conspire against you will be brought to shame and punishment.
17	★★ ★★ ★★ ★ ★	You may be a merchant, but sell not your soul for gain.
18	★ ★★ ★★ ★★ ★	It will be your Fate to pass by but not to find a treasure.
19	★ ★ ★★ ★★ ★★	Put not your trust in the fair appearance of all those whom you meet in your travels.
20	★ ★★ ★ ★★ ★★	You are sincerely beloved.
21	★ ★★ ★★ ★ ★★	Let not expense be an obstacle to the restoration of the patient's health.

22	★ ★ ★ ★ ★ ★ ★ ★	Consider well whether you ought, at present, to change your condition in life.
23	★ ★ ★ ★ ★ ★ ★ ★	Be more careful to deserve a good reputation by acting virtuously than merely avoiding the petty libels of the envious slanderer.
24	★ ★ ★ ★ ★ ★ ★ ★	It is decreed that your life will be coloured by many changes, but ultimately you shall enjoy peace and comfort.
25	★ ★ ★ ★ ★ ★ ★ ★	It signifies a gift from a far country.
26	★ ★ ★ ★ ★ ★ ★ ★	Your misfortunes are but temporary.
27	★ ★ ★ ★ ★ ★ ★ ★ ★	Point out to your children the defects of vice and they will shun it.
28	★ ★ ★ ★ ★ ★ ★ ★ ★	When you are wed, insist not too much on privilege, but let each yield a little.
29	★ ★ ★ ★ ★ ★ ★ ★ ★	Let not distrust mar your happiness.

30	★★ ★★ ★★ ★ ★★	When the time for his sojourn in a foreign land is past, he will return.
31	★ ★★ ★★ ★★ ★★	As the volcano bursts with a loud explosion, when the combustible matter is confined within its bosom, so will a nation's revenge find vent, the more their wrongs are repressed.
32	★★ ★★ ★★ ★★ ★★	The person who has wronged you will be cut off in the midst of his wickedness.

14.
Mars

1	★ ★ ★ ★ ★	The thief may be successful for a time, but in the end is certain death.
2	★★ ★ ★ ★ ★	Be exceedingly cautious in your choice of friend.
3	★ ★★ ★ ★ ★	Let your deeds deserve praise and posterity will applaud them.
4	★ ★ ★★ ★ ★	Your harvest of plenty and happiness is ready; you must reap it with the sickle of industry.
5	★ ★ ★ ★★ ★	Bless the memory of the giver!

6	★ ★ ★ ★ ★★	Be on your guard against unforseen events.
7	★★ ★★ ★ ★ ★	Be contented with your present lot.
8	★ ★★ ★★ ★ ★	Enter into no rash speculations.
9	★ ★ ★★ ★★ ★	Be warned! Henceforth, never play for money, nor money's worth.
10	★ ★ ★ ★★ ★★	When you understand thoroughly the grounds of your suit, proceed justly and in the end you will triumph.
11	★ ★ ★★ ★ ★★	If you are prudent, fortune awaits you in another country.
12	★ ★★ ★ ★★ ★	If you would see your days counted long, shun drunkenness, gluttony, and all intemperance.
13	★★ ★ ★★ ★ ★	The prisoner's release is uncertain; let some kinsman interest himself on his behalf.

14	★ ★★ ★ ★ ★★	You will marry one who has before tasted the sweets of matrimony.
15	★★ ★ ★ ★★ ★	She will have a son who will live to a great age.
16	★★ ★ ★ ★ ★★	Your friends are in good health; they have just heard news from a far country.
17	★★ ★★ ★★ ★ ★	Enemies you have, but their designs will be frustrated.
18	★ ★★ ★★ ★★ ★	Love not gold so much as to be a usurer.
19	★ ★ ★★ ★★ ★★	If you take care to acquire knowledge, it will prove a rich treasure of which no one can deprive you.
20	★ ★★ ★ ★★ ★★	When you have arrived at your place of destination, lose no time in executing your errand, and return without delay.
21	★ ★★ ★★ ★ ★★	You shall receive proof that you are beloved.

22	★ ★ ★ ★ ★ ★ ★ ★	Put faith in no advice save that of experience.
23	★ ★ ★ ★ ★ ★ ★ ★	Your husband's talents will promote him to positions of great trust.
24	★ ★ ★ ★ ★ ★ ★ ★	At one period of your existence, attempts will be made to misrepresent your conduct in the eyes of thc world.
25	★ ★ ★ ★ ★ ★ ★ ★	A peaceful life is ordained for you.
26	★ ★ ★ ★ ★ ★ ★ ★	It signifies health and happiness.
27	★ ★ ★ ★ ★ ★ ★ ★ ★	Be not discouraged though you are now engulfed in misfortune; your spirits will soon be buoyed up by prosperity.
28	★ ★ ★ ★ ★ ★ ★ ★ ★	Discourage deceit in your child; but at the same time teach him prudence, that he may not be deceived by others.
29	★ ★ ★ ★ ★ ★ ★ ★ ★	To bear and forbear is the grand secret of matrimonial happiness.

30	★★ ★★ ★★ ★ ★★	Take heed that jealousy prove not the bane of your happiness.
31	★ ★★ ★★ ★★ ★★	The traveller will return richly laden.
32	★★ ★★ ★★ ★★ ★★	While the winds are still and the air serene, the earth may quake suddenly and those on its surface be swallowed up.

15.
Pluto

1	★ ★ ★ ★ ★	After much rain, there will be a plentiful harvest.
2	★★ ★ ★ ★ ★	Exert yourself manfully to recover the property which you have lost.
3	★ ★★ ★ ★ ★	Try your friend before you trust him too deeply.
4	★ ★ ★★ ★ ★	If your deeds are evil, posterity will damn your name.
5	★ ★ ★ ★★ ★	Let not your efforts decline and you will be prosperous.

6	★ ★ ★ ★ ★★	See that you are not cheated out of your just rights.
7	★★ ★★ ★ ★ ★	If you are prudent, fear not.
8	★ ★★ ★★ ★ ★	You shall be exalted above your fellows.
9	★ ★ ★★ ★★ ★	Mind what you are about and you are sure to be successful.
10	★ ★ ★ ★★ ★★	If it will afford you pleasure to behold yourself and your family reduced from comfort to beggary — play on!
11	★ ★ ★★ ★ ★★	Plead your case before a jury of your countrymen.
12	★ ★★ ★ ★★ ★	If you remain in your own country, you may still be successful.
13	★★ ★ ★★ ★ ★	I have seen the rich man bestow all his goods to charity and have known the sun to be wholly darkened, but have never yet beheld the greyed temples and healthy vitality of an intemperate man.

14	★ ★★ ★ ★ ★★	Further woes for the unfortunate captive!
15	★★ ★ ★ ★★ ★	A rich partner, but of a very bad temper.
16	★★ ★ ★ ★ ★★	A son will be born unto you who will possess great riches.
17	★★ ★★ ★★ ★ ★	Your friends are well, but have anxiety concerning you.
18	★ ★★ ★★ ★★ ★	Be vigilant and the designs of those who would do you mischief will be defeated.
19	★ ★ ★★ ★★ ★★	Do you know that which in the shortest time will be productive of most profit to you?
20	★ ★★ ★ ★★ ★★	It is decreed that you shall find another's property; but it behoves you to restore it to the right owner.
21	★ ★★ ★★ ★ ★★	Those who are with you will guard over your safety.

22	★★ ★ ★ ★★ ★★	Give further proofs of attachment to your beloved and a due return will be made to you.
23	★★ ★ ★★ ★ ★★	The patient may look forward to many days.
24	★★ ★★ ★ ★ ★★	Many of your sex will envy you the possession of so comely and so kind a husband.
25	★★ ★★ ★ ★★ ★	The slanderous reports of your enemies will not affect the stability of your reputation.
26	★★ ★ ★★ ★★ ★	When you least expect it, a beneficial change will take place in your fortune.
27	★★ ★★ ★★ ★★ ★	It signifies recovery from illness.
28	★★ ★ ★★ ★★ ★★	Apply yourself steadily to the improvement of your fortune and success will crown your endeavours.
29	★★ ★★ ★ ★★ ★★	Train your child in the way in which he should conduct himself, and when he is old he will not depart from it.

30	★ ★ ★ ★ ★ ★ ★ ★ ★	It is folly for you to wed if you have nothing but mere beauty or love to feed upon.
31	★ ★ ★ ★ ★ ★ ★ ★ ★	Live cheerily, work merrily, watch warily, but suspect not lightly.
32	★ ★ ★ ★ ★ ★ ★ ★ ★ ★	Riches, happiness, and honour accompany the returning individual.

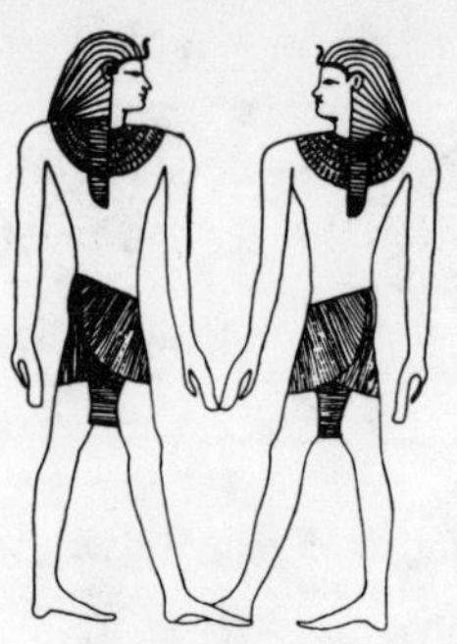

16. Gemini

1	★ ★ ★ ★ ★	Your hopes for the individual's speedy return are not well grounded.
2	★★ ★ ★ ★ ★	The governments of nations will be speedily changed.
3	★ ★★ ★ ★ ★	Punish not the delinquent too severely.
4	★ ★ ★★ ★ ★	Your friend will assuredly prove faithful to you. Is he your friend?
5	★ ★ ★ ★★ ★	Be honest and content with the praise of your contemporaries.

6	★ ★ ★ ★ ★ ★	Fail not by applying yourself industriously to fill your barns with grain, and your purse with money in case of need.
7	★ ★ ★ ★ ★ ★ ★	When you take possession of the wordly goods of the deceased, do justice to the widow and the orphan.
8	★ ★ ★ ★ ★ ★ ★	Venture not rashly.
9	★ ★ ★ ★ ★ ★ ★	Your advancement will be owing to your own deserts.
10	★ ★ ★ ★ ★ ★ ★	When you have amassed £250,000, retire!
11	★ ★ ★ ★ ★ ★ ★	Why stake your fortune, your happiness, your very existence, on the cast of a die or the turn of a card?
12	★ ★ ★ ★ ★ ★ ★	Be your own advocate.
13	★ ★ ★ ★ ★ ★ ★	When you travel, Divine Guidance will protect you.

14	★ ★★ ★ ★ ★★	You will pamper your children's children.
15	★★ ★ ★ ★★ ★	After long imprisonment he will be released.
16	★★ ★ ★ ★ ★★	Your partner will be a pattern of virtue and beauty.
17	★★ ★★ ★★ ★ ★	You shall have a son who shall inherit all his mother's accomplishments and his father's virtues.
18	★ ★★ ★★ ★★ ★	Doubt not that your friends are well and happy; they now relish the sweets of a simple but plentiful meal.
19	★ ★ ★★ ★★ ★★	The designs of the man who will become your enemy shall not prevail against you.
20	★ ★★ ★ ★★ ★★	Follow the plough.
21	★ ★★ ★★ ★ ★★	You shall assuredly find something, but it will not be of much value to you.

22	★★ ★ ★ ★★ ★★	Linger not unnecessarily on the road lest danger befall you.
23	★★ ★ ★★ ★ ★★	You are beloved but improve your opportunity, for delays are dangerous.
24	★★ ★★ ★ ★ ★★	A speedy abatement will take place in the patient's disorder.
25	★★ ★★ ★ ★★ ★	The mind and the make-up of your husband will be that of the fox; his practices are those of the wolf.
26	★★ ★ ★★ ★★ ★	The slander which is uttered against you will not be credited.
27	★★ ★★ ★★ ★★ ★	Be not dismayed if misfortune should overtake you; she will not long keep you company.
28	★★ ★ ★★ ★★ ★★	It says you have enemies who are endeavouring to render you unhappy.
29	★★ ★★ ★ ★★ ★★	Your misfortunes are not so great that your own efforts may relieve you.

30	★★ ★★ ★★ ★ ★★	Nourish the seeds of virtue in your children and doubt not that in later years they will reap the harvest of happiness.
31	★ ★★ ★★ ★★ ★★	If you would but try to make your partner happy, you shall be so likewise.
32	★★ ★★ ★★ ★★ ★★	Absence will effect no change in the sentiments of the beloved of your soul.

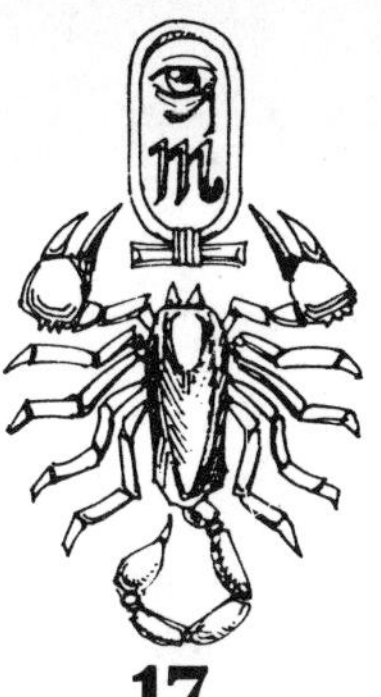

17.
Scorpio

1	★ ★ ★ ★ ★	The heart which is penetrated by love for you will prove true.
2	★★ ★ ★ ★ ★	He will soon return, to the great joy of all his friends.
3	★ ★★ ★ ★ ★	A southern nation will speedily undergo a change in its government, for the better.
4	★ ★ ★★ ★ ★	A clean corner is not the worse for being twice searched.
5	★ ★ ★ ★★ ★	Be your own friend.

6	★ ★ ★ ★ ★★	Let not a love of fame prompt you to evil deeds.
7	★★ ★★ ★ ★ ★	Your future happiness depends upon yourself.
8	★ ★★ ★★ ★ ★	What have you to do with legacies? Be industrious and thrifty.
9	★ ★ ★★ ★★ ★	Consider well before you venture farther in this scheme.
10	★ ★ ★ ★★ ★★	Your own merits will exalt you.
11	★ ★ ★★ ★ ★★	Do riches bring contentment and happiness?
12	★ ★★ ★ ★★ ★	Do not bet high.
13	★★ ★ ★★ ★ ★	Submit to no arbitration but abide by the verdict of an honest jury.

14	★ ★★ ★ ★ ★★	Your journey will be prosperous if guided by prudence.
15	★★ ★ ★ ★★ ★	You shall be termed venerable; see that your long life is spent usefully.
16	★★ ★ ★ ★ ★★	The bolts will be drawn, the door opened, and the chain will be broken.
17	★★ ★★ ★★ ★ ★	Your partner will not be handsome, but there will be no other cause for dislike.
18	★ ★★ ★★ ★★ ★	A son will be born unto you who shall possess much power.
19	★ ★ ★★ ★★ ★★	The health of your friend requires a physician's aid; he peruses a letter just received which gives much satisfaction.
20	★ ★★ ★ ★★ ★★	An enemy will endeavour to mar your prospects but he will be taken in the net which he hath spread for you.
21	★ ★★ ★★ ★ ★★	Seek not the honours nor the dangers of the field.

22	★★ ★ ★ ★★ ★★	A good-humoured partner will be a treasure which your eyes will delight to look upon.
23	★★ ★ ★★ ★ ★★	The companions of your travels will be a shield against every danger.
24	★★ ★★ ★ ★ ★★	You have the love of others beside that of the darling of your heart.
25	★★ ★★ ★ ★★ ★	Let not the patient be afflicted by melancholy forebodings.
26	★★ ★ ★★ ★★ ★	Your husband will sit in high places.
27	★★ ★★ ★★ ★★ ★	Evil reports will be uttered against you, but in due time the slanderer will be discovered and brought to punishment.
28	★★ ★ ★★ ★★ ★★	Remember well that the lessons which you receive in misfortune's school may be useful to you when you are prosperous.
29	★★ ★★ ★ ★★ ★★	It signifies that you will soon hear agreeable news.

30	★★ ★★ ★★ ★ ★★	Be patient now, and in the future, prudent; only thus can you attain prosperity and happiness.
31	★ ★★ ★★ ★★ ★★	Chastise the child when he does evil, and in the end he will have cause to bless your name.
32	★★ ★★ ★★ ★★ ★★	Examine strictly the disposition of your intended partner, and if it accord with your own, fear not but happiness will attend you both.

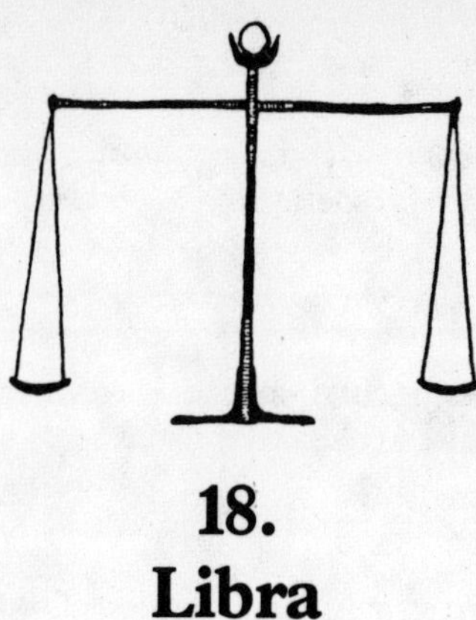

18.
Libra

1	★ ★ ★ ★ ★	Those who observe truly the vows that have been sworn at the altar need not fear unhappiness.
2	★★ ★ ★ ★ ★	Question not the faithfulness of your beloved.
3	★ ★★ ★ ★ ★	He will not return at the time expected.
4	★ ★ ★★ ★ ★	The present age teems with events of much political import.
5	★ ★ ★ ★★ ★	Seek and you shall find.

6	★ ★ ★ ★ ★★	Trust not even a friend with a secret which ought to remain within your own breast.
7	★★ ★★ ★ ★ ★	Though the present generation may flatter you, the succeeding one may not be so courteous.
8	★ ★★ ★★ ★ ★	Place not your happiness in stores of gold and silver; but in all your dealings preserve your conscience pure and undefiled.
9	★ ★ ★★ ★★ ★	Hope for the best!
10	★ ★ ★ ★★ ★★	Be not puffed up with the success which may be your lot.
11	★ ★ ★★ ★ ★★	As the Nile produces abundant harvests by its annual overflow, so will the good-will of a friend produce you advancement, fortune, and honour.
12	★ ★★ ★ ★★ ★	Your speculations will be generally successful.
13	★★ ★ ★★ ★ ★	A lucky hit may make your fortune; if so, play no more.

14	★ ★★ ★ ★ ★★	Endeavour to accommodate all differences by the private arbitration of mutual friends.
15	★★ ★ ★ ★★ ★	You shall remain where you now reside.
16	★★ ★ ★ ★ ★★	You shall live long; let not your years be passed ingloriously.
17	★★ ★★ ★★ ★ ★	The fettered will soon be free!
18	★ ★★ ★★ ★★ ★	A rich partner is ordained for you.
19	★ ★ ★★ ★★ ★★	You shall have a daughter who will possess a noble mind and amiable manners.
20	★ ★★ ★ ★★ ★★	The friend for whom you inquire is in good health and is now locked in the arms of sleep.
21	★ ★★ ★★ ★ ★★	See that your present friends do not become your determined foes.

22	★★ ★ ★ ★★ ★★	Take medication when there is need, but presume not to give it to others.
23	★★ ★ ★★ ★ ★★	Be industrious and place no reliance on daydreams.
24	★★ ★★ ★ ★ ★★	Boast not on the riches which you carry with you lest they be coveted by others.
25	★★ ★★ ★ ★★ ★	You are adored but lose not your advantage by inattention or procrastination.
26	★★ ★ ★★ ★★ ★	Let strict attention be paid to the directions given by the medical attendant.
27	★★ ★★ ★★ ★★ ★	Your husband shall have rules and direction over affairs of great importance.
28	★★ ★ ★★ ★★ ★★	Give not the slandered an opportunity of injuring your reputation.
29	★★ ★★ ★ ★★ ★★	When you have enough, therewith be content and seek not to enlarge your store by venturing further.

30	★★ ★★ ★★ ★ ★★	It signifies plenty of everything which gold can purchase.
31	★ ★★ ★★ ★★ ★★	Though you are poor and needy, purchase not prosperity by any sacrifice of honesty or honour; Fortune's wheel is constantly turning.
32	★★ ★★ ★★ ★★ ★★	Neglect no opportunity of cultivating the minds of your children and their journey through life will be virtuous and happy.

19.
Leo

1	★ ★ ★ ★ ★	Commit the several members of your family to the care of the all-seeing God; He will protect.
2	★★ ★ ★ ★ ★	Mutual love will secure prosperity and real happiness.
3	★ ★★ ★ ★ ★	Be as constant to your beloved as she is to you, and you may be happy.
4	★ ★ ★★ ★ ★	The individual will return unexpectedly.
5	★ ★ ★ ★★ ★	The wise man will make provision against every change that may take place.

6	★ ★ ★ ★ ★★	Make proper inquiries and they will lead to detection.
7	★★ ★★ ★ ★ ★	Show your friend, by good treatment of him, that it is in his interest to be faithful to you.
8	★ ★★ ★★ ★ ★	Desire not to attain immortality by the vices of reckless ambition.
9	★ ★ ★★ ★★ ★	Brood not over your misfortunes, but exert yourself for the future.
10	★ ★ ★ ★★ ★★	Good fortune is in store for you.
11	★ ★ ★★ ★ ★★	Keep your own counsel and success will attend you.
12	★ ★★ ★ ★★ ★	Neglect not the opportunities which may be offered to you for they will lead to great advancement.
13	★★ ★ ★★ ★ ★	A partner in your business would ruin you.

<table>
<tr><td>14</td><td>★
★★
★
★
★★</td><td>Never throw good money after bad.</td></tr>
<tr><td>15</td><td>★★
★
★
★★
★</td><td>With the blessing of God you shall gain your cause.</td></tr>
<tr><td>16</td><td>★★
★
★
★
★★</td><td>Wander not far from your home.</td></tr>
<tr><td>17</td><td>★★
★★
★★
★
★</td><td>Providence watches over you and will lengthen your days if you avoid the sin of drunkenness.</td></tr>
<tr><td>18</td><td>★
★★
★★
★★
★</td><td>After a short time, all anxiety for the prisoner will cease.</td></tr>
<tr><td>19</td><td>★
★
★★
★★
★★</td><td>You will be exceedingly fortunate in your marriage.</td></tr>
<tr><td>20</td><td>★
★★
★
★★
★★</td><td>A son will be born who, if he receives not timely correction, may prove a source of trouble to you.</td></tr>
<tr><td>21</td><td>★
★★
★★
★
★★</td><td>The object of your solicitude is as well in health as you could wish, and is now engaged in domestic occupations.</td></tr>
</table>

22	★★ ★ ★ ★★ ★★	Beware of treachery! Nothing further may be now revealed to you.
23	★★ ★ ★★ ★ ★★	Cultivate your talents and adopt a profession supported by fees.
24	★★ ★★ ★ ★ ★★	You may; but be not disappointed if it is not of great value.
25	★★ ★★ ★ ★★ ★	Set out one day soon or go later than you had previously intended.
26	★★ ★ ★★ ★★ ★	Your love is mutual, but endeavours will be made to cause dissension between you.
27	★★ ★★ ★★ ★★ ★	To ensure recovery, the patient's mind must be kept in cheerful mood by the conversation of those who are most beloved.
28	★★ ★ ★★ ★★ ★★	You shall wed a man of high birth, but little fortune.
29	★★ ★★ ★ ★★ ★★	Let justice and prudence be the guardians of your reputation.

30	★★ ★★ ★★ ★ ★★	The early part of your career will be subject to change but in your old age you shall enjoy uninterrupted happiness.
31	★ ★★ ★★ ★★ ★★	It warns you to beware of danger.
32	★★ ★★ ★★ ★★ ★★	Sit not down under your misfortune, wringing your hands and accusing the justice of providence, but be up and doing and fortune will again smile upon you.

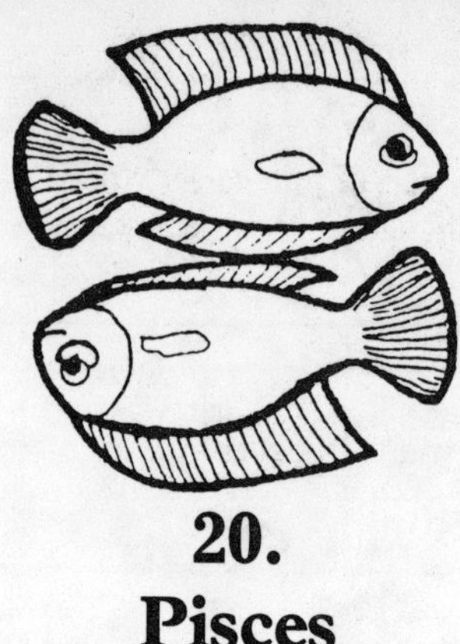

20.
Pisces

1	★ ★ ★ ★ ★	As the tall column is exalted above the petty ruins which surround its base so shall you rise superior to your present misfortunes.
2	★★ ★ ★ ★ ★	If you have been prudent and just, your family will follow your example and be happy.
3	★ ★★ ★ ★ ★	Confidence in each other will ensure happiness.
4	★ ★ ★★ ★ ★	The heart of your beloved will find room for no other object but yourself.
5	★ ★ ★ ★★ ★	The individual will return at the time you expect him.

6	★ ★ ★ ★ ★★	If the season be unfavourable, let your efforts be the greater.
7	★★ ★★ ★ ★ ★	Despair not of recovering your goods.
8	★ ★★ ★★ ★ ★	Wrangle not with your friend about trifles, else you may forfeit his assistance in matters of great import.
9	★ ★ ★★ ★★ ★	Do justice rather for justice' sake than to be praised in future ages.
10	★ ★ ★ ★★ ★★	Anticipate not misfortunes before their time.
11	★ ★ ★★ ★ ★★	The money which will be left you will not compensate your anxiety.
12	★ ★★ ★ ★★ ★	Seek the counsel of one wiser than yourself.
13	★★ ★ ★★ ★ ★	Eminence is attained by the proper culture of great talents and position; your lot is cast between both.

14	★ ★★ ★ ★ ★★	Take a partner, but be not yourself a sleeping one.
15	★★ ★ ★ ★★ ★	Visit a gaming house; behold the despair of the player who has just lost all, and then play.
16	★★ ★ ★ ★ ★★	You shall be foiled by your opponent's cunning devices.
17	★★ ★★ ★★ ★ ★	In a foreign land strangers will protect and cherish you.
18	★ ★★ ★★ ★★ ★	Desire not so much the length of days, but to improve the time which God gives you on earth.
19	★ ★ ★★ ★★ ★★	The prisoner ought to sue for pardon and mercy.
20	★ ★★ ★ ★★ ★★	By this marriage you will soon obtain great property.
21	★ ★★ ★★ ★ ★★	Your progeny shall be both male and female; they will be the staff and comfort of old age.

22	★★ ★ ★ ★★ ★★	The friend whom you enquire after is in excellent health, and is now engaged in conversation with a relative.
23	★★ ★ ★★ ★ ★★	An enemy will try to circumvent you but he will be foiled in his attempt.
24	★★ ★★ ★ ★ ★★	Follow the bent of your own inclinations.
25	★★ ★★ ★ ★★ ★	Domestic happiness will be of more value to you than the contents of ten thousand mines of gold, silver and precious stones.
26	★★ ★ ★★ ★★ ★	Be not dismayed if you should meet with danger; it will not affect you if you are resolute.
27	★★ ★★ ★★ ★★ ★	The heartbeat of your beloved is responsive to the anxious throbbings of your own.
28	★★ ★ ★★ ★★ ★★	It is useless to look for relief from medicine unless it be skilfully applied.
29	★★ ★★ ★ ★★ ★★	The man whom you wed shall have great power; teach him to use it rightly.

30	★★ ★★ ★★ ★ ★★	When you are unjustly accused, your innocence will thereby be confirmed, and the slanderers will be confounded.
31	★ ★★ ★★ ★★ ★★	Expect not to pass through life without a mixture of good and evil.
32	★★ ★★ ★★ ★★ ★★	It portends a happy union between a man and woman, who have long loved each other.

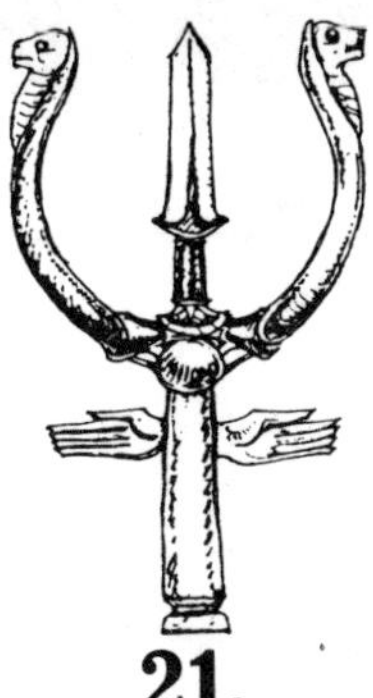

21.
Neptune

1	★ ★ ★ ★ ★	Your nightly visions indicate good fortune for you.
2	★ ★ ★ ★ ★ ★	Your misfortunes shall soon have an end.
3	★ ★ ★ ★ ★ ★	Instruct your children, provide them a good example, and fear not for their happiness.
4	★ ★ ★ ★ ★ ★	The marriage will prove both prosperous and happy.
5	★ ★ ★ ★ ★ ★	Another will endeavour to supplant you in the affections of the being whom you tenderly love.

6	★ ★ ★ ★ ★★	The individual cannot return at present.
7	★★ ★★ ★ ★ ★	The earth will be fertilized by abundance of rain.
8	★ ★★ ★★ ★ ★	Are you certain that it has been stolen?
9	★ ★ ★★ ★★ ★	Reckon not much on the friendship of any man.
10	★ ★ ★ ★★ ★★	Fulfil the duties of your station and care not for the unprofitableness of future fame.
11	★ ★ ★★ ★ ★★	If you continue virtuous, you shall be happy.
12	★ ★★ ★ ★★ ★	Depend not on the caprice of youth.
13	★★ ★ ★★ ★ ★	Look before you leap.

14	★ ★★ ★ ★ ★★	When you enjoy prosperity and honour, feel for the misfortunes of your former friends.
15	★★ ★ ★ ★★ ★	Have a strict eye over those who eat your bread.
16	★★ ★ ★ ★ ★★	The companion of cheats and thieves, even with a fortune, is never respected.
17	★★ ★★ ★★ ★ ★	Venture freely in your next cause and gain will crown your wishes.
18	★ ★★ ★★ ★★ ★	Await your Fate at home; it will be better for you.
19	★ ★ ★★ ★★ ★★	Longevity is a curse to those who misspend life.
20	★ ★★ ★ ★★ ★★	The prisoner will still pass many days in confinement.
21	★ ★★ ★★ ★ ★★	Your matrimonial connections will not produce much happiness.

22	★★ ★ ★ ★★ ★★	Sons and daughters will be the reward of the love which you bear each other.
23	★★ ★ ★★ ★ ★★	Your friend is now in the act of paying a visit, and is both well and happy.
24	★★ ★★ ★ ★ ★★	You have little cause to dread the rage of any enemy who shall come against you.
25	★★ ★★ ★ ★★ ★	Be one of your country's defenders.
26	★★ ★ ★★ ★★ ★	One of your kindred shall find articles of great value.
27	★★ ★★ ★★ ★★ ★	The object of your journey will be attained without hazard.
28	★★ ★ ★★ ★★ ★★	The heart of your beloved wavers between you and another; improve the opportunities that will be offered you.
29	★★ ★★ ★ ★★ ★★	The patient may still hope for health and long life.

<table>
<tr><td>30</td><td>★★
★★
★★
★
★★</td><td>Your husband's position will be exalted.</td></tr>
<tr><td>31</td><td>★
★★
★★
★★
★★</td><td>You innocence will uphold you in the day of trial and the tongue of the slanderer will be forever silenced.</td></tr>
<tr><td>32</td><td>★★
★★
★★
★★
★★</td><td>Your voyage through life will at first be boisterous, but the tempest will cease and propitious winds will waft you into the haven of independence.</td></tr>
</table>

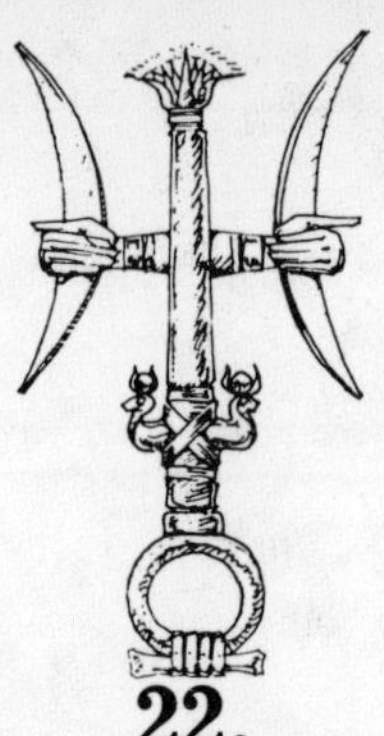

22.
Uranus

1	★ ★ ★ ★ ★	You shall be subject to a frequent change of residence.
2	★★ ★ ★ ★ ★	Your dream signifies that you should bestow some of your goods to charity.
3	★ ★★ ★ ★ ★	Be not dispirited by misfortunes; they will vanish as the thick mist is dissipated by the genial rays of the reviving sun.
4	★ ★ ★★ ★ ★	As you sow, so shall your children reap.
5	★ ★ ★ ★★ ★	Let no petty bickerings disturb the happiness of the married state.

<table>
<tr><td>6</td><td>★
★
★
★
★★</td><td>Your beloved will not cease to pray for your speedy return.</td></tr>
<tr><td>7</td><td>★★
★★
★
★
★</td><td>He will return in due season.</td></tr>
<tr><td>8</td><td>★
★★
★★
★
★</td><td>Expect a plentiful harvest.</td></tr>
<tr><td>9</td><td>★
★
★★
★★
★</td><td>The thief shall ultimately be detected.</td></tr>
<tr><td>10</td><td>★
★
★
★★
★★</td><td>Sad is his Fate who relies solely on the friendship and good-will of others.</td></tr>
<tr><td>11</td><td>★
★
★★
★
★★</td><td>While you seek to obtain fame, take heed that infamy may not be your reward.</td></tr>
<tr><td>12</td><td>★
★★
★
★★
★</td><td>As the sun revives the flowers of the field, so will prosperity in business make your heart glad.</td></tr>
<tr><td>13</td><td>★★
★
★★
★
★</td><td>Blessed is he who expects little, for he will not be disappointed.</td></tr>
</table>

14	★ ★★ ★ ★ ★★	Examine yourself strictly, whether you ought not abandon your present intentions.
15	★★ ★ ★ ★★ ★	When you enjoy the favour of powerful men, let not your pride inflate.
16	★★ ★ ★ ★ ★★	You will be the architect of your own fortune; depend on no created being.
17	★★ ★★ ★★ ★ ★	Be not intoxicated with good fortune at first; this is the bait which is thrown out by the hunter to allure his prey.
18	★ ★★ ★★ ★★ ★	If you are tricked out of your upper garment, throw not your under one away to recover it.
19	★ ★ ★★ ★★ ★★	Let not your inordinate desire of amassing wealth carry you into foreign climes.
20	★ ★★ ★ ★★ ★★	Desire not to attain old age if your mind be not well stored with knowledge; no wretch is so truly wretched as the ignorant old man.
21	★ ★★ ★★ ★ ★★	Someone will pity and release the prisoner.

22	★★ ★ ★ ★★ ★★	You will have every cause to love your partner.
23	★★ ★ ★★ ★ ★★	Numerous offspring will be born to you; if you raise them up properly, their virtues will reward your anxious toil.
24	★★ ★★ ★ ★ ★★	Your friend is free from all bodily affliction and expects to receive a letter or news from you.
25	★★ ★★ ★ ★★ ★	In a contest which may soon take place, you shall be victorious over your avowed enemies.
26	★★ ★ ★★ ★★ ★	You would cut a sorry figure in the pulpit.
27	★★ ★★ ★★ ★★ ★	Chase not after shadows for you may thereby lose your substance.
28	★★ ★ ★★ ★★ ★★	If you meet danger; face it boldly and do not be daunted by appearances.
29	★★ ★★ ★ ★★ ★★	Fear not that another will supplant you in the affections of the beloved of your soul.

30	★★ ★★ ★★ ★ ★★	The patient's mind must not be affected by depressing reports.
31	★ ★★ ★★ ★★ ★★	Peace, plenty, and happiness will attend your marriage with the beloved of your heart.
32	★★ ★★ ★★ ★★ ★★	Deal openly, prudently, and honestly, and you may avoid the tongue of the slandered.

23.
Mercury

1	★ ★ ★ ★ ★	But few persons escape the malicious tongue of gossip.
2	★ ★ ★ ★ ★ ★	You shall meet with few upheavals.
3	★ ★ ★ ★ ★ ★	The interpretation is that you shall receive a message of importance.
4	★ ★ ★ ★ ★ ★	Your own efforts will enable you to overcome every misfortune which may happen.
5	★ ★ ★ ★ ★ ★	Lead your children in the paths of righteousness and when you are gone they will not depart from it.

6	★ ★ ★ ★ ★★	Happiness depends solely on the affection and forbearance of both parties.
7	★★ ★★ ★ ★ ★	There is danger in long absence from the object of your affection.
8	★ ★★ ★★ ★ ★	Matters of importance prevent his return.
9	★ ★ ★★ ★★ ★	A revolutionary spirit is abroad among the nations of the earth.
10	★ ★ ★ ★★ ★★	Be patient and every circumstance will be developed
11	★ ★ ★★ ★ ★★	If a man professes never-ceasing friendship to you, at least doubt his sincerity.
12	★ ★★ ★ ★★ ★	Tarnish not your laurels by unjust deeds.
13	★★ ★ ★★ ★ ★	Carry yourself prudently and justly and you will surely be happy.

<table>
<tr><td>14</td><td>★
★★
★
★
★★</td><td>Let not disappointment mar your efforts in your calling.</td></tr>
<tr><td>15</td><td>★★
★
★
★★
★</td><td>Fortune will attend you.</td></tr>
<tr><td>16</td><td>★★
★
★
★
★★</td><td>When you are in the zenith of your power, let not unjust deeds procure your downfall.</td></tr>
<tr><td>17</td><td>★★
★★
★★
★
★</td><td>Do not pay large interest for money in your business.</td></tr>
<tr><td>18</td><td>★
★★
★★
★★
★</td><td>If you play, play fair and see that others do the same.</td></tr>
<tr><td>19</td><td>★
★
★★
★★
★★</td><td>There is great hindrance to your present success in law matters.</td></tr>
<tr><td>20</td><td>★
★★
★
★★
★★</td><td>Emigration from your native land will but retard your fortune.</td></tr>
<tr><td>21</td><td>★
★★
★★
★
★★</td><td>Vain mortal! What would you? Grey hair and longevity are the reward for temperance and virtue.</td></tr>
</table>

22	★★ ★ ★ ★★ ★★	Try to unlock the dungeon by means of a golden key.
23	★★ ★ ★★ ★ ★★	Be wary and this marriage may prove very fortunate.
24	★★ ★★ ★ ★ ★★	She shall have a son who in his youth will be admired, and in his old age respected.
25	★★ ★★ ★ ★★ ★	Your friends labour under no bodily affliction but they are not free from cares concerning worldly matters.
26	★★ ★ ★★ ★★ ★	Your enemies are powerless and unworthy of your regard.
27	★★ ★★ ★★ ★★ ★	On this subject take the advice last given you by your best friend.
28	★★ ★ ★★ ★★ ★★	In this, fortune has not marked you for her favourite.
29	★★ ★★ ★ ★★ ★★	On your journey, fear not that from each stop a robber will spring upon you but pursue your way steadily.

30	★★ ★★ ★★ ★ ★★	Success will attend your anxious hopes if you are discreet in this matter.
31	★ ★★ ★★ ★★ ★★	A speedy cure will depend much on the patience with which the afflicted bears this present illness.
32	★★ ★★ ★★ ★★ ★★	Your husband will be a man well willed, with a house well filled, and a farm well tilled.

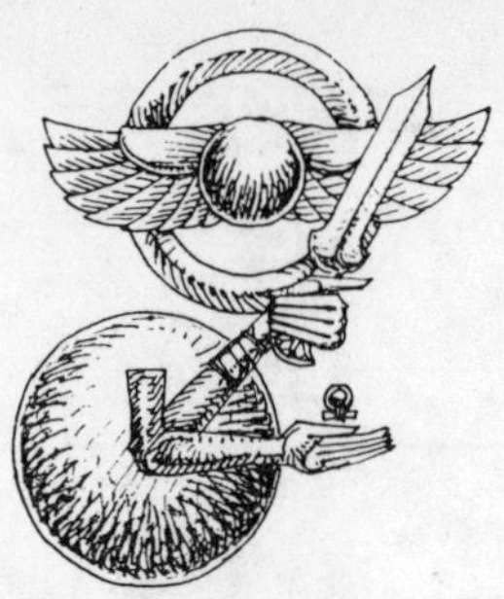

24.
Sun/Mars

1	★ ★ ★ ★ ★	Your husband will be learned, his temper good, and his complexion fair.
2	★ ★ ★ ★ ★ ★	Your maligners will, sooner or later, be overwhelmed with shame and disgrace.
3	★ ★ ★ ★ ★ ★	If you stay at home you shall meet with few changes.
4	★ ★ ★ ★ ★ ★	Your dream portends ill luck to your enemies.
5	★ ★ ★ ★ ★ ★	Your misfortunes will cease to overpower you.

6	★ ★ ★ ★ ★★	Have more anxiety to bequeath knowledge than riches to your children and they will be happy.
7	★★ ★★ ★ ★ ★	This union will produce real happiness.
8	★ ★★ ★★ ★ ★	Be not neglectful and your beloved will remain true.
9	★ ★ ★★ ★★ ★	The traveller will speedily revisit his own country and kindred.
10	★ ★ ★ ★★ ★★	Despotism will speedily be overturned in a country long oppressed by illiterate, indolent and luxurious strangers.
11	★ ★ ★★ ★ ★★	Make diligent inquiries amongst the members of your house.
12	★ ★★ ★ ★★ ★	Rely more on the actions than on the promises of your friends.
13	★★ ★ ★★ ★ ★	Only the good deeds of the virtuous will be held in esteem by posterity.

14	★ ★★ ★ ★ ★★	Your misfortunes will vanish and you shall be happy.
15	★★ ★ ★ ★★ ★	Follow your calling diligently and be not a legacy hunter.
16	★★ ★ ★ ★ ★★	Rejoice at the fortune which is ordained for you and therewith be content.
17	★★ ★★ ★★ ★ ★	When you enjoy the favour of the mighty men of the earth, take heed that you are not ruined by a flattering tongue.
18	★ ★★ ★★ ★★ ★	Deal honestly and trust to God for success.
19	★ ★ ★★ ★★ ★★	Mind your business and forsake the gaming table.
20	★ ★★ ★ ★★ ★★	Do not pay large fees in this suit.
21	★ ★★ ★★ ★ ★★	In a far country shall you find treasure.

22	★★ ★ ★ ★★ ★★	If you are temperate in your appetites, cleanly in your person, and just in your dealings, the winter of your years will run smoothly.
23	★★ ★ ★★ ★ ★★	The captive will suffer no bodily affliction.
24	★★ ★★ ★ ★ ★★	This marriage will add to your welfare and happiness.
25	★★ ★★ ★ ★★ ★	She will have a son with a contrary disposition; but it is your business to correct and counsel him aright.
26	★★ ★ ★★ ★★ ★	Your friend is in good health and has some thoughts of going on a journey.
27	★★ ★★ ★★ ★★ ★	You have enemies who speak ill of you and who would otherwise injure you.
28	★★ ★ ★★ ★★ ★★	Deal in books and be prosperous.
29	★★ ★★ ★ ★★ ★★	A good name will prove to you a treasure of great value; see you lose it not.

30	★★ ★★ ★★ ★ ★★	Tarry not unnecessarily on your journey; delays may prove dangerous to your safety.
31	★ ★★ ★★ ★★ ★★	A return of affection is at present doubtful, but perseverance and attention will ensure you success.
32	★★ ★★ ★★ ★★ ★★	Let the patient's mind be soothed by the kind and ready attentions of friends and the happiest result may be anticipated.

25.
Virgo

1	★ ★ ★ ★ ★	The patient may recover, but in case of the worst, due preparation ought to be made for the tomb.
2	★ ★ ★ ★ ★ ★	Your husband's temper will be good and he will make you happy if you do not attempt to rule over him.
3	★ ★ ★ ★ ★ ★	Were you chaste as ice and pure as snow, you cannot escape false charges against you.
4	★ ★ ★ ★ ★ ★	As the frail bark is tossed on the ocean so will you be on the stormy sea of life, but in the end you shall enter the haven of prosperity.
5	★ ★ ★ ★ ★ ★	It signifies that you must take heed to avoid danger.

6	★ ★ ★ ★ ★★	Unlooked-for fortune and happiness await you.
7	★★ ★★ ★ ★ ★	Teach not your children to be covetous and they will be both contented and happy.
8	★ ★★ ★★ ★ ★	Marriage, when prudently undertaken, is the happiest state into which man can enter.
9	★ ★ ★★ ★★ ★	Fear not that the darling of your heart will prove unfaithful.
10	★ ★ ★ ★★ ★★	He will not stay long.
11	★ ★ ★★ ★ ★★	A nation accustomed to changes has still to undergo a great one.
12	★ ★★ ★ ★★ ★	Blame not your servant unjustly.
13	★★ ★ ★★ ★ ★	Friends are so scarce that when found they are to be valued above all price.

14	★ ★★ ★ ★ ★★	Of what enjoyment is fame if you have no fortune!
15	★★ ★ ★ ★★ ★	As the drooping plant is refreshed by the dew of heaven, so will your heart be gladdened by sudden prosperity.
16	★★ ★ ★ ★ ★★	Divide your inheritance with those who have an equal right with you.
17	★★ ★★ ★★ ★ ★	Rely not too much on present good fortune.
18	★ ★★ ★★ ★★ ★	Use no servile means to procure advancement; you shall be exalted without their aid.
19	★ ★ ★★ ★★ ★★	The eye of a master is worth his two hands.
20	★ ★★ ★ ★★ ★★	Avoid everything that savours of hell.
21	★ ★★ ★★ ★ ★★	Your expectations from the law are vain; you shall not succeed.

22	★★ ★ ★ ★★ ★★	Await your happy destiny at home.
23	★★ ★ ★★ ★ ★★	It is utter vanity in you to desire long life if your daily habits tend to destroy it.
24	★★ ★★ ★ ★ ★★	Cherish and support the poor captive who will soon be unfettered.
25	★★ ★★ ★ ★★ ★	Content will render this union a complete paradise.
26	★★ ★ ★★ ★★ ★	You shall be blessed with sons and daughters; but forget not that the tree preserves the fashion which has been given to it when a sapling.
27	★★ ★★ ★★ ★★ ★	A slight disorder affects the person concerning whom you are solicitous, but it will soon pass away.
28	★★ ★ ★★ ★★ ★★	The barbed arrow which shall be shot at you by a secret enemy will recoil on his own head.
29	★★ ★★ ★ ★★ ★★	If you like remnants, use the needle.

30	★★ ★★ ★★ ★ ★★	Treasures are but rarely found; throw not your time away in searching after them.
31	★ ★★ ★★ ★★ ★★	Adopt yourself to the customs of those whom you meet on your journey and you shall meet with little annoyance.
32	★★ ★★ ★★ ★★ ★★	You shall, in time, attain to greater happiness in this matter than you can at present begin to hope for.

26.
Venus

1	★ ★ ★ ★ ★	There is much harmony in the love which you and the darling of your heart bear towards each other.
2	★★ ★ ★ ★ ★	The patient will assuredly recover from the present illness.
3	★ ★★ ★ ★ ★	Your husband will be rich; but his constant aim will be to bear sway over you and to keep you under his thumb.
4	★ ★ ★★ ★ ★	The evil reports of your enemies will not affect your character.
5	★ ★ ★ ★★ ★	Few changes await you.

6	★ ★ ★ ★ ★ ★	The interpretation is that if you observe any blemish in your own conduct, you should lose no time in correcting it.
7	★ ★ ★ ★ ★ ★ ★	Shrink not from encountering whatever may occur to you; what you now deem misfortune may ultimately turn to your advantage.
8	★ ★ ★ ★ ★ ★ ★	Instill honour and honesty into the minds of your children and fear not for their prosperity and happiness.
9	★ ★ ★ ★ ★ ★ ★	Let no one interfere in the domestic feuds of married people; if left alone they will soon subside, and the parties will be happy as before.
10	★ ★ ★ ★ ★ ★ ★	Forget not to keep up written communication with the beloved of your heart.
11	★ ★ ★ ★ ★ ★ ★	Let preparation be made for his speedy return from abroad.
12	★ ★ ★ ★ ★ ★ ★	Where insolent oppression reigns, where tears water the soil, and where sighs fan the scanty harvest, the freed husbandman will sit under his fig tree revelling in the joys of abundance.
13	★ ★ ★ ★ ★ ★ ★	Accuse not the innocent rashly.

14	★ ★★ ★ ★ ★★	If you are joined with another in a compact to act wickedly, expect not that he will prove faithful to you.
15	★★ ★ ★ ★★ ★	The applauses of the wicked are unprofitable, but the praises of the just are like honey which drops from the comb.
16	★★ ★ ★ ★ ★★	Correct those faults in yourself which you see in others and you shall be happy and gain immeasurably.
17	★★ ★★ ★★ ★ ★	The legacy that shall be bequeathed unto you will not profit you much if you spend it foolishly.
18	★ ★★ ★★ ★★ ★	Lose not everything by rash speculation!
19	★ ★ ★★ ★★ ★★	Be not servile in adversity nor despotic in prosperity.
20	★ ★★ ★ ★★ ★★	Yes! If you do steadily avoid the habits of squander.
21	★ ★★ ★★ ★ ★★	Better even sleep away your time than spend it in ruining yourself or others.

22	★★ ★ ★ ★★ ★★	Endeavour to settle all differences in a private manner.
23	★★ ★ ★★ ★ ★★	Set forth upon the ocean of the depths or of the heights without fear.
24	★★ ★★ ★ ★ ★★	The wicked old man is a wretch who tastes of hell before his time. Would you be aged and wicked too? Go to! Rather let the sapling wither than the tree be rotten!
25	★★ ★★ ★ ★★ ★	Visit the captive who is in affliction; but his woes will soon be turned into joy.
26	★★ ★ ★★ ★★ ★	You shall marry a very worthy personage who will inherit considerable property.
27	★★ ★★ ★★ ★★ ★	As the protecting oak is encircled by the tender ivy, so shall a numerous race of sons and daughters claim your paternal regard.
28	★★ ★ ★★ ★★ ★★	Your friend is in good health at the present time; he is in the act of bestowing charity.
29	★★ ★★ ★ ★★ ★★	Act with caution and you shall undoubtedly triumph over a powerful enemy.

30	★★ ★★ ★★ ★ ★★	Obtain an insight into two trades in which the hands are principally employed; reflect on both for a week, and follow that which you are so inclined.
31	★ ★★ ★★ ★★ ★★	Be as industrious as you are now covetous and great riches will be your reward.
32	★★ ★★ ★★ ★★ ★★	Be not affected by the petty inconveniences which you may meet with; otherwise if you should be beset with real dangers, you shall not have the courage to face them.

27.
Sagittarius

1	★ ★ ★ ★ ★	Go well armed and equipped and dispute not with your companions on the way, and the journey will be safe and prosperous.
2	★★ ★ ★ ★ ★	Your image is ever before the eyes of your beloved.
3	★ ★★ ★ ★ ★	The patient's disorder will yield to proper remedies.
4	★ ★ ★★ ★ ★	You shall be united to a man whose complexion is dark, but whose features are handsome.
5	★ ★ ★ ★★ ★	The evil report of your enemies will recoil on their own heads.

6	★ ★ ★ ★ ★★	Prosperity will succeed misfortune.
7	★★ ★★ ★ ★ ★	It signifies that your conduct requires amendment.
8	★ ★★ ★★ ★ ★	Fear not that misfortunes will continue to pursue you.
9	★ ★ ★★ ★★ ★	Those whom you are anxious about will be prosperous and happy.
10	★ ★ ★ ★★ ★★	Let each concede to the other in matters of trifling import, and both will be happy.
11	★ ★ ★★ ★ ★★	Give your beloved no cause to prove unfaithful to you.
12	★ ★★ ★ ★★ ★	He must still remain a stranger for a short season.
13	★★ ★ ★★ ★ ★	The air which has long been filled with the sighs of oppression will soon resound with shouts of 'Liberty!'

14	★ ★★ ★ ★ ★★	Be secret and examine each person singly.
15	★★ ★ ★ ★★ ★	If you expect that a companion in wickedness will prove a faithful friend, you are deceived.
16	★★ ★ ★ ★ ★★	Enter upon no design of which you have not well considered whether it will accrue to your honour.
17	★★ ★★ ★★ ★ ★	Avoid the snares of your enemies.
18	★ ★★ ★★ ★★ ★	Although you inherit testamentary property, still be industrious and frugal.
19	★ ★ ★★ ★★ ★★	If you have enough earthly goods, be content and run no risks.
20	★ ★★ ★ ★★ ★★	Interest will procure you positions of great trust.
21	★ ★★ ★★ ★ ★★	Avoid, cards, women and wine — and prosper.

22	★★ ★ ★ ★★ ★★	Your risks are great, your chance of gaining is small, and in the end, perhaps you will lose all.
23	★★ ★ ★★ ★ ★★	Your gain, at best, will be trivial.
24	★★ ★★ ★ ★ ★★	Be steady in your resolution to turn your back on your native shores.
25	★★ ★★ ★ ★★ ★	So bear yourself toward your children and your kinsfolk that they may watch over and protect you when age wears you down and your powers fail you.
26	★★ ★ ★★ ★★ ★	The captive will be released, but let him beware of again falling into the clutches of power.
27	★★ ★★ ★★ ★★ ★	You shall have an honourable, young, and handsome partner.
28	★★ ★ ★★ ★★ ★★	Sons will be born unto you; train them in their youth in the way they should go, and when they are old they will not depart from it.
29	★★ ★★ ★ ★★ ★★	Your friend is in the enjoyment of good health but is not entirely divested of cares.

<table>
<tr><td>30</td><td>★ ★
★ ★
★ ★
★
★ ★</td><td>See that your conduct be such that men may love and not hate you.</td></tr>
<tr><td>31</td><td>★
★ ★
★ ★
★ ★
★ ★</td><td>Choose a business in which the hands, rather than the head, are employed.</td></tr>
<tr><td>32</td><td>★ ★
★ ★
★ ★
★ ★
★ ★</td><td>When you find a treasure, teach your tongue to be silent and see that you make good use of your riches.</td></tr>
</table>

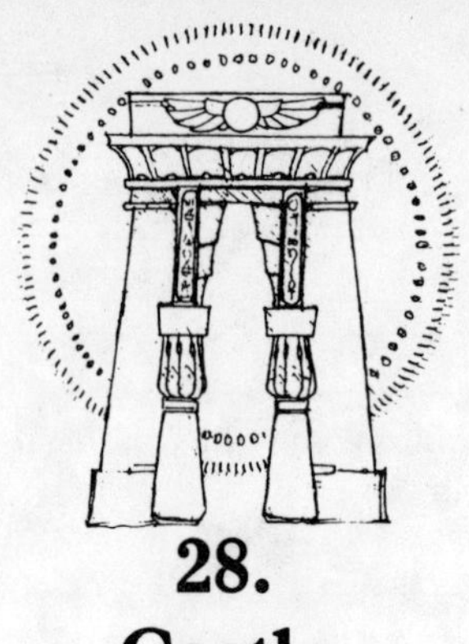

28.
Castle

1	★ ★ ★ ★ ★	If you dig up your fields with the plough of industry, you will find a treasure which will reward your labour.
2	★★ ★ ★ ★ ★	Your journey will be prosperous.
3	★ ★★ ★ ★ ★	You may hope to gain a place in the affections of the darling of your soul.
4	★ ★ ★★ ★ ★	The pain with which the patient is afflicted will soon be terminated.
5	★ ★ ★ ★★ ★	Your husband will be exalted to a high station.

6	★ ★ ★ ★ ★★	Your detractors are busy, but they will be baffled in their endeavours to injure you.
7	★★ ★★ ★ ★ ★	Great changes await you but they will not much affect your future fortune.
8	★ ★★ ★★ ★ ★	The signification is that good luck will befall you.
9	★ ★ ★★ ★★ ★	Misfortunes may be your lot in the beginning, but in the end will be sweetness and happiness.
10	★ ★ ★ ★★ ★★	Fail not to instruct your children in all knowledge which may be set for them and they will assuredly profit in the end.
11	★ ★ ★★ ★ ★★	Mutual forbearance is the strongest bond of matrimonial happiness.
12	★ ★★ ★ ★★ ★	The affections of the being whom you love will be placed on none other but yourself.
13	★★ ★ ★★ ★ ★	He will come back with abundance of riches and knowledge.

14	★ ★ ★ ★ ★ ★ ★	He who rules the kings of the earth and who terrifies the nations with the sound of his arms will be abased and speedily cut off.
15	★ ★ ★ ★ ★ ★ ★	Be sure of your grounds before you enter on a prosecution.
16	★ ★ ★ ★ ★ ★ ★	Choose your friends only from among the virtuous and fear no treachery.
17	★ ★ ★ ★ ★ ★ ★ ★	The approval of your Creator is more profitable than the empty applause of men.
18	★ ★ ★ ★ ★ ★ ★ ★	Be select in the choice of your friends and the future will be happier than the past.
19	★ ★ ★ ★ ★ ★ ★ ★	Though you inherit houses and lands, to what end does it profit if you are unwise?
20	★ ★ ★ ★ ★ ★ ★ ★	Impediments will start up which you dreamed not of.
21	★ ★ ★ ★ ★ ★ ★ ★	Be honourable and honest in your dealings and you shall be greatly exalted.

22	★★ ★ ★ ★★ ★★	You will find the benefit of neither giving nor taking long credit.
23	★★ ★ ★★ ★ ★★	Leave off play as the clock strikes twelve; after that hour there is no luck for you.
24	★★ ★★ ★ ★ ★★	Do you expect to snatch the burning oil from the devouring flames? Think no more of rescuing your goods out of the fire of the law if once it fed upon them.
25	★★ ★★ ★ ★★ ★	You shall visit distant regions where gold abounds. In your prosperity forget not the widow and the orphan.
26	★★ ★ ★★ ★★ ★	Do not desire old age if you too freely indulge carnal appetites.
27	★★ ★★ ★★ ★★ ★	Captivity, anxiety, suspense, liberty, and joy, will rapidly succeed each other.
28	★★ ★ ★★ ★★ ★★	You shall marry your equal in worth and fortune. Be content and happy.
29	★★ ★★ ★ ★★ ★★	As the roses bloom upon the parent tree, so will sons and daughters grace you by their beauty.

No.	Stars	Answer
30	★★ ★★ ★★ ★ ★★	The objects of your anxious inquiry are well; they are equally solicitous regarding your welfare.
31	★ ★★ ★★ ★★ ★★	You will be envied but it should be your constant care that even your enemies shall have cause to admire your virtues.
32	★★ ★★ ★★ ★★ ★★	Choose not a business which depends on the whim and luxury of the era in which you live.

29.
Capricorn

1	★ ★ ★ ★ ★	From small beginnings, by industry, can one attain the highest position in the land. Go you and do likewise.
2	★★ ★ ★ ★ ★	Lose not time from your business in looking after hidden treasures.
3	★ ★★ ★ ★ ★	Prosperity will attend your travels but you must still be prudent.
4	★ ★ ★★ ★ ★	Rejoice! You are truly beloved.
5	★ ★ ★ ★★ ★	The patient's disorder will soon be greatly alleviated.

6	★ ★ ★ ★ ★★	Your husband will possess great riches.
7	★★ ★★ ★ ★ ★	Let your reputation be founded in virtues and you need not dread ill will and enmity slung by Fate.
8	★ ★★ ★★ ★ ★	Fear not that fortune will desert you.
9	★ ★ ★★ ★★ ★	It portends kindness and charity to your poor friends.
10	★ ★ ★ ★★ ★★	After rain comes sunshine.
11	★ ★ ★★ ★ ★★	As you hope for happiness for your children, lead them in the paths of virtue and honour.
12	★ ★★ ★ ★★ ★	Misfortunes may cloud the dawn of matrimony, but the evening will be serene and happy.
13	★★ ★ ★★ ★ ★	Doubt not the vows of love which have been made to you.

14	★ ★★ ★ ★ ★★	A certain circumstance prevents his immediate return.
15	★★ ★ ★ ★★ ★	Those who have long sighed for freedom shall soon attain it.
16	★★ ★ ★ ★ ★★	When you have discovered the thief, see that his punishment be proportionate to his crime.
17	★★ ★★ ★★ ★ ★	If you expect your friend to be true, be true to him.
18	★ ★★ ★★ ★★ ★	If your deeds are just, fear not but that future generations will hold your memory in esteem.
19	★ ★ ★★ ★★ ★★	A man's happiness depends entirely on the company which he keeps.
20	★ ★★ ★ ★★ ★★	Forget not that the goods which you inherit are not of your own earning; therefore remember the poor in the days of your prosperity.
21	★ ★★ ★★ ★ ★★	Before you build, reckon the cost of your house.

22	★★ ★ ★ ★★ ★★	Your reputation will be exalted above your fellow.
23	★★ ★ ★★ ★ ★★	Rise early, mind your business, be regular in your accounts, and prosper.
24	★★ ★★ ★ ★ ★★	Never drink until the game is ended.
25	★★ ★★ ★ ★★ ★	It will be vanity in you to expect success from your possessions.
26	★★ ★ ★★ ★★ ★	Fortune will favour you in your own country.
27	★★ ★★ ★★ ★★ ★	Longevity and sensual gratification are incompatible; think not of enjoying both.
28	★★ ★ ★★ ★★ ★★	The captive will at length escape and triumph over his enemies.
29	★★ ★★ ★ ★★ ★★	You will marry a person with whom you will have much comfort.

30	★★ ★★ ★★ ★ ★★	You shall have three lovely daughters; instruct and watch over them, as you would over the apple of your eye.
31	★ ★★ ★★ ★★ ★★	Your friend enjoys health and happiness; he is in the act of economic counsel.
32	★★ ★★ ★★ ★★ ★★	Heed not the feeble and impotent attempts of him who will attempt to hurt you.

30.
Aries

1	★ ★ ★ ★ ★	You have enemies who if not restrained by fear of the laws would plunge a dagger in your heart.
2	★★ ★ ★ ★ ★	The soldier's bayonet has sometimes given place to the Field-Marshal's baton.
3	★ ★★ ★ ★ ★	The treasure you will find will be a partner whose affectionate heart will share your happiness and sympathize in all your sorrows.
4	★ ★ ★★ ★ ★	No ill luck will befall you.
5	★ ★ ★ ★★ ★	There is no lack of regard on the part of your beloved.

6	★ ★ ★ ★ ★★	The patient's illness will yield to proper remedies.
7	★★ ★★ ★ ★ ★	You shall wed a man of much substance.
8	★ ★★ ★★ ★ ★	You shall be well spoken of.
9	★ ★ ★★ ★★ ★	Be shrewd and your changes will bring you nearer to the happiness destined for you.
10	★ ★ ★ ★★ ★★	It portends danger if you are not cautious.
11	★ ★ ★★ ★ ★★	The clouds on your brow will be dispersed by beams of fortune and happiness.
12	★ ★★ ★ ★★ ★	Restrain your children when they indulge in wicked courses, and when you are gathered unto your fathers, they will have cause to bless your name.
13	★★ ★ ★★ ★ ★	Fear not that misfortune will attend this marriage.

14	★ ★★ ★ ★ ★★	Your own fidelity and that of your beloved will be rewarded with happiness.
15	★★ ★ ★ ★★ ★	The stranger will return, but not speedily.
16	★★ ★ ★ ★ ★★	Tyranny will soon be engulfed in the abyss of its own iniquity.
17	★★ ★★ ★★ ★ ★	By perseverance only shall you recover your goods.
18	★ ★★ ★★ ★★ ★	When you ask advice from your friend, relate not to him your story by halves lest in concealing the matter from him you suffer in the end.
19	★ ★ ★★ ★★ ★★	In future ages shall your name be cited as a pattern for rising generations if you are the benefactor of mankind.
20	★ ★★ ★ ★★ ★★	Avoid places of ill repute and be happy.
21	★ ★★ ★★ ★ ★★	Your own earnings will prove much sweeter than the largest inheritance.

No.	Stars	Oracle
22	★★ ★ ★ ★★ ★★	Be exceedingly cautious in your present speculations.
23	★★ ★ ★★ ★ ★★	Be true in your present trust and you shall have affairs of much importance committed to your care.
24	★★ ★★ ★ ★ ★★	The industrious man is seldom the fortunate one.
25	★★ ★★ ★ ★★ ★	Confine yourself to games wherein you may overcome your rival by ingenuity and fair play.
26	★★ ★ ★★ ★★ ★	You will soon obtain what you least expect.
27	★★ ★★ ★★ ★★ ★	If you go far abroad, your kinsmen at home will not deal justly by you — tarry not by the way.
28	★★ ★ ★★ ★★ ★★	Old age never commands respect unless it be allied with virtue; would you be old and detested too?
29	★★ ★★ ★ ★★ ★★	The captive will live to see his enemies punished.

30	★★ ★★ ★★ ★ ★★	Your partner will, if used well, go through every danger for you.
31	★ ★★ ★★ ★★ ★★	As the parent trunk giveth up a part of its nourishment to the tender shoots which spring from its sides, so will sons and daughters require your aid and protection.
32	★★ ★★ ★★ ★★ ★★	Fear not for the health of your friends; they are in expectation that you will send them some small matter whereby they may keep you in remembrance.

31.
Aquarius

1	★ ★ ★ ★ ★	Your friends are well and sleep soundly in the mansion of content and happiness.
2	★ ★ ★ ★ ★ ★	Your enemies will not have power to harm you.
3	★ ★ ★ ★ ★ ★	Make a bold effort to run for high office.
4	★ ★ ★ ★ ★ ★	It will not be your fortune to discover hidden treasures.
5	★ ★ ★ ★ ★ ★	Let prudence be your guide and you will reach your journey's end in safety.

6	★ ★ ★ ★ ★★	The beloved of your soul adores you in secret.
7	★★ ★★ ★ ★ ★	Let every means be used for the restoration of health.
8	★ ★★ ★★ ★ ★	The good temper of your husband will make you happy.
9	★ ★ ★★ ★★ ★	Waste not your time by seeking for the good report of every man.
10	★ ★ ★ ★★ ★★	Man that is born of woman is born to trouble — the sparks fly upwards.
11	★ ★ ★★ ★ ★★	It signifies that you ought not to trust another with affairs which you can manage yourself.
12	★ ★★ ★ ★★ ★	Let not your misfortunes unnerve you, but prepare yourself for happier times.
13	★★ ★ ★★ ★ ★	When the upright man sleeps under the sod, happiness and prosperity will attend his offspring.

14	★ ★★ ★ ★ ★★	A marriage founded on greed is seldom a happy one.
15	★★ ★ ★ ★★ ★	Consult your own heart whether you ought to have exacted a vow of fidelity.
16	★★ ★ ★ ★ ★★	The stranger will return soon.
17	★★ ★★ ★★ ★ ★	The wings of the eagle of the north will be clipped and his talons blunted.
18	★ ★★ ★★ ★★ ★	It is necessary for you to bear your loss with fortitude.
19	★ ★ ★★ ★★ ★★	One act of unconditional friendship should cancel the remembrance of a thousand flaws.
20	★ ★★ ★ ★★ ★★	Abuse not the power which the Lord gave you and your name will be hailed with rapture in future ages.
21	★ ★★ ★★ ★ ★★	Your misfortunes will soon terminate.

22	★ ★ ★ ★ ★ ★ ★ ★	Fear not that your own industry will procure you a sufficient provision.
23	★ ★ ★ ★ ★ ★ ★ ★	Let prudence and justice be your handmaidens and all your undertakings will prove successful.
24	★ ★ ★ ★ ★ ★ ★ ★	Kick not down the ladder which raises you.
25	★ ★ ★ ★ ★ ★ ★ ★	A penny saved is a penny got; a word to the wise is enough.
26	★ ★ ★ ★ ★ ★ ★ ★	Effect no mortgate to pay a gambling debt.
27	★ ★ ★ ★ ★ ★ ★ ★ ★	Your hope is vain, justice is blind to your claims, and Fortune shuns you.
28	★ ★ ★ ★ ★ ★ ★ ★ ★	Distribute the wealth you gain abroad justly and charitably at home.
29	★ ★ ★ ★ ★ ★ ★ ★ ★	To arrive at old age you must avoid the causes of premature decay.

30	★★ ★★ ★★ ★ ★★	Liberty will be proclaimed to the captive.
31	★ ★★ ★★ ★★ ★★	A handsome good-natured partner, a bag of gold, and a carriage.
32	★★ ★★ ★★ ★★ ★★	A son will be born unto you who will not disappoint the hope which you shall entertain respecting him.

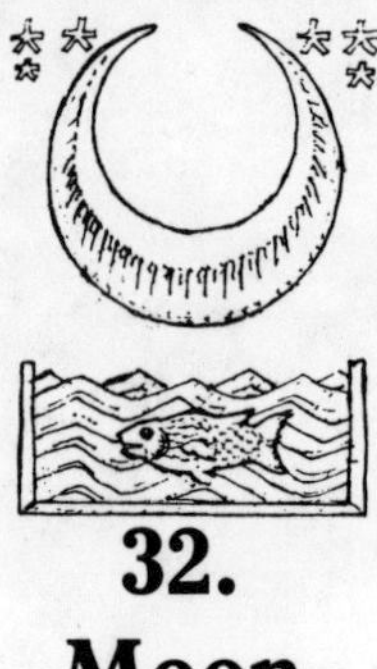

32.
Moon

1	★ ★ ★ ★ ★	Your wife will bless you with a large offspring and she will be among them, as the queen of night among the stars of the heavens.
2	★ ★ ★ ★ ★ ★	Those concerning whom you are anxious are well and happy; they now enjoy the sweet nectar of conversation.
3	★ ★ ★ ★ ★ ★	You have, but fear not that they will have power to injure you.
4	★ ★ ★ ★ ★ ★	Write over your doorway 'Ironing done here'.
5	★ ★ ★ ★ ★ ★	The silver and gold which has been buried in the earth will forever be hidden from your view.

6	★ ★ ★ ★ ★★	When you go forth from your dwelling, no harm will overtake you.
7	★★ ★★ ★ ★ ★	Your love will meet its due return.
8	★ ★★ ★★ ★ ★	While there is life, there is hope; let no means be left untried to cure the disorder.
9	★ ★ ★★ ★★ ★	An honourable man will wed you.
10	★ ★ ★ ★★ ★★	Your reputation will, in a small degree, be affected by detraction.
11	★ ★ ★★ ★ ★★	Many scenes will be presented before your eyes.
12	★ ★★ ★ ★★ ★	It says that if you procrastinate, evil will attend you.
13	★★ ★ ★★ ★ ★	Your misfortunes ought to be your future monitors; take heed and prosperity will attend you.

No.	Stars	Answer
14	★ ★★ ★ ★ ★★	To be happy, it is necessary only to be virtuous; teach this to your children and they will benefit.
15	★★ ★ ★ ★★ ★	Care not so much for abundance of gold and silver with your partner as stores of virtue and prudence and your marriage will be a happy one.
16	★★ ★ ★ ★ ★★	Take it not greatly to heart if the being you now dote upon should prove fickle.
17	★★ ★★ ★★ ★ ★	The individual's return will be hailed with joy.
18	★ ★★ ★★ ★★ ★	The storm of revolution will rage throughout the earth for a time, but in the end, peace and plenty will be diffused among the nations.
19	★ ★ ★★ ★★ ★★	When you have recovered your goods, take care to secure them for the future.
20	★ ★★ ★ ★★ ★★	Let not interested persons have so much power over you as to cause distrust or discord between your friend and you.
21	★ ★★ ★★ ★ ★★	Let not your desire of making your name live forever urge you on to deeds of cruelty and lust.

22	★★ ★ ★ ★★ ★★	Happiness and misery are merely relative; therefore, make not yourself unhappy over trivial matters.
23	★★ ★ ★★ ★ ★★	Be not intoxicated with good fortune when it arrives.
24	★★ ★★ ★ ★ ★★	Rely not on showy appearances.
25	★★ ★★ ★ ★★ ★	Good deeds will advance you to honour.
26	★★ ★ ★★ ★★ ★	Envy not your industrious neighbour, but steadily follow his example.
27	★★ ★★ ★★ ★★ ★	Beware of foul play.
28	★★ ★ ★★ ★★ ★★	Does the wolf tamely relinquish his prey or the fox his booty? How then do you expect to rescue your goods from the fangs of the man of law?
29	★★ ★★ ★ ★★ ★★	Fear not for your journey — it will be prosperous.

30	★★ ★★ ★★ ★ ★★	Let temperance be your nurse, labour your physician, and you will need none other, for health will be the companion of old age.
31	★ ★★ ★★ ★★ ★★	Speedy release for the prisoner!
32	★★ ★★ ★★ ★★ ★★	Your partner will possess houses and lands.

APPENDIX

Questions which may be put to the Oracle and which will be truly answered according to the hieroglyphical indications of the Cosmos

1 Inform me of any specifics relating to the woman I shall marry.

2 Will the prisoner be released or continue in bondage?

3 Shall I live to an old age?

4 Shall I travel far by sea or land or reside far from my present home?

5 Shall I be involved in litigation and if so, shall I gain or lose my cause?

6 Shall I make or mar my fortune by gambling?

7 Shall I ever be able to retire from business with a fortune?

8 Shall I be eminent and advance in my pursuits?

9 Shall I be successful in my present undertaking?

10 Shall property come to me through inheritance or testament?

11 Shall I spend this year happier than the last?

12 Will my name be immortalized and will posterity applaud it?

13 Will the friend upon whom I most rely prove faithful or treacherous?

14 Will the stolen property be recovered and will the thief be detected?

15 What is the aspect of the seasons and what political changes are likely to take place?

16 Shall I accept the stranger's offer?

17 Will my beloved prove true in my absence?

18 Will the marriage about to take place be happy and prosperous?

19 After my death will my children be happy?

20 Shall I ever recover from my present misfortunes?

21 Does my dream signify good luck or misfortune?

22 Will it be my lot to experience great changes in this life?

23 Will my reputation be at all or much affected by deceit or misrepresentation?

24 Inform me of any specifics relating to my future husband.

25 Shall the patient recover from the illness?

26 Does the person whom I love love me?

27 Shall my intended journey be blessed or unfortunate?

28 Shall I ever find a treasure?

29 What trade or profession should I follow?

30 Have I any or many enemies?

31 Are absent friends in good health and what is their present involvement?

32 Will the expected child be a son or a daughter?

Table of Questions and Oracles

No	1	2	3	4	5	6	7	8	9	10	11	12	13	14	15	16	17	18	19	20	21	22	23	24	25	26	27	28	29	30	31	32
Q	* * * * *	* * * * * *	* * * * * *	* * * * * *	* * * * * *	* * * * * *	* * * * * * *	* * * * * * *	* * * * * * *	* * * * * * *	* * * * * * *	* * * * * * *	* * * * * * *	* * * * * * *	* * * * * * *	* * * * * * *	* * * * * * * *	* * * * * * * *	* * * * * * * *	* * * * * * * *	* * * * * * * *	* * * * * * * *	* * * * * * * *	* * * * * * * *	* * * * * * * *	* * * * * * * *	* * * * * * * * *	* * * * * * * * *	* * * * * * * * *	* * * * * * * * *	* * * * * * * * *	* * * * * * * * * *
1	♀☽	✕	♋	∼	✕✕	♃	♉	≣	★	💀	θ	Δ	♄	♂	♇	♊	♏	♎	♌	♓	♆	♅	☿	☉♂	♍	♀	♐	🏰	♑	♈	♒	☽
2	✕	♋	∼	✕✕	♃	♉	≣	★	💀	θ	Δ	♄	♂	♇	♊	♏	♎	♌	♓	♆	♅	☿	☉♂	♍	♀	♐	🏰	♑	♈	♒	☽	♀☽
3	♋	∼	✕✕	♃	♉	≣	★	💀	θ	Δ	♄	♂	♇	♊	♏	♎	♌	♓	♆	♅	☿	☉♂	♍	♀	♐	🏰	♑	♈	♒	☽	♀☽	✕
4	∼	✕✕	♃	♉	≣	★	💀	θ	Δ	♄	♂	♇	♊	♏	♎	♌	♓	♆	♅	☿	☉♂	♍	♀	♐	🏰	♑	♈	♒	☽	♀☽	✕	♋
5	✕✕	♃	♉	≣	★	💀	θ	Δ	♄	♂	♇	♊	♏	♎	♌	♓	♆	♅	☿	☉♂	♍	♀	♐	🏰	♑	♈	♒	☽	♀☽	✕	♋	∼
6	♃	♉	≣	★	💀	θ	Δ	♄	♂	♇	♊	♏	♎	♌	♓	♆	♅	☿	☉♂	♍	♀	♐	🏰	♑	♈	♒	☽	♀☽	✕	♋	∼	✕✕
7	♉	≣	★	💀	θ	Δ	♄	♂	♇	♊	♏	♎	♌	♓	♆	♅	☿	☉♂	♍	♀	♐	🏰	♑	♈	♒	☽	♀☽	✕	♋	∼	✕✕	♃
8	≣	★	💀	θ	Δ	♄	♂	♇	♊	♏	♎	♌	♓	♆	♅	☿	☉♂	♍	♀	♐	🏰	♑	♈	♒	☽	♀☽	✕	♋	∼	✕✕	♃	♉
9	★	💀	θ	Δ	♄	♂	♇	♊	♏	♎	♌	♓	♆	♅	☿	☉♂	♍	♀	♐	🏰	♑	♈	♒	☽	♀☽	✕	♋	∼	✕✕	♃	♉	≣
10	💀	θ	Δ	♄	♂	♇	♊	♏	♎	♌	♓	♆	♅	☿	☉♂	♍	♀	♐	🏰	♑	♈	♒	☽	♀☽	✕	♋	∼	✕✕	♃	♉	≣	★
11	θ	Δ	♄	♂	♇	♊	♏	♎	♌	♓	♆	♅	☿	☉♂	♍	♀	♐	🏰	♑	♈	♒	☽	♀☽	✕	♋	∼	✕✕	♃	♉	≣	★	💀
12	Δ	♄	♂	♇	♊	♏	♎	♌	♓	♆	♅	☿	☉♂	♍	♀	♐	🏰	♑	♈	♒	☽	♀☽	✕	♋	∼	✕✕	♃	♉	≣	★	💀	θ
13	♄	♂	♇	♊	♏	♎	♌	♓	♆	♅	☿	☉♂	♍	♀	♐	🏰	♑	♈	♒	☽	♀☽	✕	♋	∼	✕✕	♃	♉	≣	★	💀	θ	Δ
14	♂	♇	♊	♏	♎	♌	♓	♆	♅	☿	☉♂	♍	♀	♐	🏰	♑	♈	♒	☽	♀☽	✕	♋	∼	✕✕	♃	♉	≣	★	💀	θ	Δ	♄
15	♇	♊	♏	♎	♌	♓	♆	♅	☿	☉♂	♍	♀	♐	🏰	♑	♈	♒	☽	♀	✕	♋	∼	✕✕	♃	♉	≣	★	💀	θ	Δ	♄	♂

No	1	2	3	4	5	6	7	8	9	10	11	12	13	14	15	16	17	18	19	20	21	22	23	24	25	26	27	28	29	30	31	32
Q	* * * * *	* * * * * *	* * * * * *	* * * * * *	* * * * * *	* * * * * *	* * * * * * *	* * * * * * *	* * * * * * *	* * * * * * *	* * * * * * *	* * * * * * *	* * * * * * *	* * * * * * *	* * * * * * *	* * * * * * *	* * * * * * * *	* * * * * * * *	* * * * * * * *	* * * * * * * *	* * * * * * * *	* * * * * * * *	* * * * * * * *	* * * * * * * *	* * * * * * * *	* * * * * * * *	* * * * * * * * *	* * * * * * * * *	* * * * * * * * *	* * * * * * * * *	* * * * * * * * *	* * * * * * * * * *
16	♊	♏	♎	♌	♓	♆	♅	☿	☉♂	♍	♀	♐	♜	♑	♈	♒	☽	♀☽	✕	♋	~	✕✕	♃	♉	Ħ	★	☠	θ	Δ	♄	♂	♇
17	♏	♎	♌	♓	♆	♅	☿	☉♂	♍	♀	♐	♜	♑	♈	♒	☽	♀☽	✕	♋	~	✕✕	♃	♉	Ħ	★	☠	θ	Δ	♄	♂	♇	♊
18	♎	♌	♓	♆	♅	☿	☉♂	♍	♀	♐	♜	♑	♈	♒	☽	♀☽	✕	♋	~	✕✕	♃	♉	Ħ	★	☠	θ	Δ	♄	♂	♇	♊	♏
19	♌	♓	♆	♅	☿	☉♂	♍	♀	♐	♜	♑	♈	♒	☽	♀☽	✕	♋	~	✕✕	♃	♉	Ħ	★	☠	θ	Δ	♄	♂	♇	♊	♏	♎
20	♓	♆	♅	☿	☉♂	♍	♀	♐	♜	♑	♈	♒	☽	♀☽	✕	♋	~	✕✕	♃	♉	Ħ	★	☠	θ	Δ	♄	♂	♇	♊	♏	♎	♌
21	♆	♅	☿	☉♂	♍	♀	♐	♜	♑	♈	♒	☽	♀☽	✕	♋	~	✕✕	♃	♉	Ħ	★	☠	θ	Δ	♄	♂	♇	♊	♏	♎	♌	♓
22	♅	☿	☉♂	♍	♀	♐	♜	♑	♈	♒	☽	♀☽	✕	♋	~	✕✕	♃	♉	Ħ	★	☠	θ	Δ	♄	♂	♇	♊	♏	♎	♌	♓	♆
23	☿	☉♂	♍	♀	♐	♜	♑	♈	♒	☽	♀☽	✕	♋	~	✕✕	♃	♉	Ħ	★	☠	θ	Δ	♄	♂	♇	♊	♏	♎	♌	♓	♆	♅
24	☉♂	♍	♀	♐	♜	♑	♈	♒	☽	♀☽	✕	♋	~	✕✕	♃	♉	Ħ	★	☠	θ	Δ	♄	♂	♇	♊	♏	♎	♌	♓	♆	♅	☿
25	♍	♀	♐	♜	♑	♈	♒	☽	♀☽	✕	♋	~	✕✕	♃	♉	Ħ	★	☠	θ	Δ	♄	♂	♇	♊	♏	♎	♌	♓	♆	♅	☿	☉♂
26	♀	♐	♜	♑	♈	♒	☽	♀☽	✕	♋	~	✕✕	♃	♉	Ħ	★	☠	θ	Δ	♄	♂	♇	♊	♏	♎	♌	♓	♆	♅	☿	☉♂	♍
27	♐	♜	♑	♈	♒	☽	♀☽	✕	♋	~	✕✕	♃	♉	Ħ	★	☠	θ	Δ	♄	♂	♇	♊	♏	♎	♌	♓	♆	♅	☿	☉♂	♍	♀
28	♜	♑	♈	♒	☽	♀☽	✕	♋	~	✕✕	♃	♉	Ħ	★	☠	θ	Δ	♄	♂	♇	♊	♏	♎	♌	♓	♆	♅	☿	☉♂	♍	♀	♐
29	♑	♈	♒	☽	♀☽	✕	♋	~	✕✕	♃	♉	Ħ	★	☠	θ	Δ	♄	♂	♇	♊	♏	♎	♌	♓	♆	♅	☿	☉♂	♍	♀	♐	♜
30	♈	♒	☽	♀☽	✕	♋	~	✕✕	♃	♉	Ħ	★	☠	θ	Δ	♄	♂	♇	♊	♏	♎	♌	♓	♆	♅	☿	☉♂	♍	♀	♐	♜	♑
31	♒	☽	♀☽	✕	♋	~	✕✕	♃	♉	Ħ	★	☠	θ	Δ	♄	♂	♇	♊	♏	♎	♌	♓	♆	♅	☿	☉♂	♍	♀	♐	♜	♑	♈
32	☽	♀☽	✕	♋	~	✕✕	♃	♉	Ħ	★	☠	θ	Δ	♄	♂	♇	♊	♏	♎	♌	♓	♆	♅	☿	☉♂	♍	♀	♐	♜	♑	♈	♒

Key to the Oracles

Oracle Reading

NAME: ______________________ DATE: ______________

Vertical Lines

1 ______________________

2 ______________________

3 ______________________

4 ______________________

5 ______________________

Question No. ________ Oracle No. ________

Column of Stars

____

____

____

____

____

No. ________

ANSWER: ______________________

____

____

Oracle Reading

NAME: ______________________ DATE: ______________

Vertical Lines	Column of Stars
1 ______________________	______________
2 ______________________	______________
3 ______________________	______________
4 ______________________	______________
5 ______________________	______________
Question No. __________ Oracle No. __________	No. __________

ANSWER: ______________________________________

____

____